*My Rabbi
Doesn't Make
House Calls*

ALBERT VORSPAN

My Rabbi
Doesn't Make
House Calls

DOUBLEDAY & COMPANY, INC., GARDEN CITY, NEW YORK   1969

818.5
V

Library of Congress Catalog Card Number 69–20083
Copyright © 1969 by Albert Vorspan
All Rights Reserved
Printed in the United States of America

This book is for the buoyant Jewish people, unwilling to bow before adversity, unquenchable in their passion for life, unafraid to laugh at the world, and even themselves.

Preface

Every few months a national magazine comes out with a bombshell article on how American Jews are vanishing. The article always cites the low Jewish birth rate, the growing rate of intermarriage and the alienation of Jewish college students. The reaction is always the same. Jews panic. The magazine sells out by morning. Jewish masochism is briefly gratified. For months, the synagogue pulpits of the land resound with dire sermons on the imminent disappearance of the Jews while the congregants, experiencing a mild sensation of déjà vu, sigh sadly, facing the end—once again—with resigned fortitude. Then the article vanishes; the Jews plod on.

This has been going on for three thousand years. It will go on for another three thousand years. If you are a gambling man, put your chips on the Jews. No people has been counted out so often—and always outlives those who bet against them. Believe it—Jews are here for the duration. They are the greatest survivors in history. (Have you seen any Babylonians lately?)

The main point the alarmists seem to make is that Jews were always able to overcome adversity, but America is killing them with kindness. The argument is that persecution and poverty toughened the Jewish fiber; but can Jews survive freedom and affluence in America?

In listening to rabbis and others in this lament, one almost senses a belief that it takes occasional crises, conflict, and a modicum of anti-Semitism to keep Jews straight. The alarmists fear that Jews are so small a group (5,500,000 in America) that they are bound to be assimilated into the magnetic field of America. I demur. In fact, I think the reverse is happening. Far from Jewish life assimilating in America, America is becoming Jewish.

It's *in* to be Jewish in America. Jewish themes compete with homosexuality and race for dominion of the Broadway stage. In fact, a recent off-Broadway play, plucking all the strings in the bow, had a Jewish faggot going steady with a black man he called "African Queen." *Fiddler on the Roof* is an American epic. Jewish authors —Roth, Pinter, Salinger, Bellows, Elkin, Malamud—dominate our literary scene. Millions of Americans kept *The Chosen*, a story of Chasidic Jews in Williamsburg, at the top of the best-seller list for months. Harry Golden turns Jewish nostalgia into Gentile tears and American gold. A talented goy named James Michener writes *The Source* and becomes a spiritual Semite. A bevy of Jewish comedians and wits—Jack Benny, George Burns, Jerry Lewis, Sam Levenson, Milton Berle, Mort Sahl, Tom Lehrer, Alan King, Red Buttons, Buddy Hackett, Jackie Mason (a former Orthodox rabbi yet) and many others—

keep America laughing with an Americanized Jewish humor. For such Jewish humor is as American as apple pie and you don't have to be Jewish to purvey it. The Lebanese Catholic, Danny Thomas, proves that.

Yiddish words have invaded the language of American humor and culture. Such words as "chutzpa," "shlemiel," "nebbish," "farblunjet," "shlepp," "kvetch," "mazel tov," "meshuga" are now practically red, white and blue. Jewish ballast is *de rigueur* in balanced political tickets in most big cities. Politicians must eat cheese blintzes on television when they hit the political trail. You do not have to be Jewish to eat Levy's rye bread, to become a herring mayvin, or to be a Jewish mother. General Moshe Dayan is an American folk hero to the United States Congress and the American people. An Arab spokesman at the U.N. accused the Israelis of chutzpa! Jewish foods —cheese blintzes, lox, bagels, and latkes—anchor the nation. Zionism is losing its hold on most Jews; its chief bastion in America today is the United States Congress. Yiddish is dying out among Jews; it is IN with America— five hundred Yiddish words now brighten Webster's Unabridged Dictionary.

Even Jewish values permeate American life. Jews have always revered education. Jewish motivation for education is so fierce it hurts. America as a whole is now getting that way; Negro mothers are now behaving like Jewish mothers and our educators had better get with it. The Jewish Bible is a detailed war on poverty; America has now proclaimed that war in modern guise. Sargent Shriver used to tell audiences that the war on poverty is a translation into the American idiom of Maimonides' Ladder of Charity. Jewish fund-raising techniques, with their high pressure and high yield, are now as American as the New York Yankees. So Jewish life is not being lost in America. In a plural America, it is helping to Judaize America. So stop kvetching; you're not vanishing.

Some non-Jews even convert to Judaism. In recent years some very spectacular conversions have taken place —Sammy Davis, Elizabeth Taylor, the late Marilyn Monroe. Thousands of less dramatic conversions are recorded each year, perhaps even balancing out the leakage by intermarriage. But it is not necessary to convert, although converts are accepted. Being Jewish is a warm, tangy, zesty experience; it's like sibling rivalry nationalized. Jews are a many-splendored people. But you don't have to sign up or take an oath or a vow. You can become a spiritual, psychological or sympathetic Jew even though you're as goyish as Nelson Rockefeller or Y. A. Tittle. All you need is this book (you must buy it; I don't care whether you read it or not), and mail the following certificate to the author along with the tops of two close Jewish friends. If you begin to understand how Jews think, feel, behave and respond to stimuli, you will be a better, more sensitive person. And you will know a hell of a lot more than I do.

Perhaps this is the time to state my qualifications for writing this book. I have worked professionally for some twenty years in the application of Jewish social action toward the achievement of a just America and a peaceful world. I believe that Jewish values represent a goad to human conscience, and I think these values are finely balanced with the finest of American traditions. Humor has always been the salt and savor of Jewish life, and Jews have never been afraid to laugh at their own foibles and follies. This is especially true in the bracing freedom that Jews enjoy in America.

Of course, there are always public relations-conscious Jews who cluck at public expressions of self-criticism and whisper: "What will the Gentiles say?" Such supersensitive Jews are always ready to report Sholom Aleichem to the Anti-Defamation League, to unfrock Rabbi Herbert Tarr (*Heaven Help Us*) and to denounce the modern Jewish satirist as a traitor to his folk. But ironic humor has kept Jews sane in an insane world, and the timorous do not prevail. I tried this manuscript out on eighteen random Jews. Fifteen said it should be burned; two said the author should be; one was too burned to say anything. Nobody is perfect.

As a Jewish bureaucrat, I have survived approximately thirteen thousand meetings. I have taken three tons of conscientious notes at these meetings; fortunately, I have lost them all. I have, however, retained my doodling. Without the doodles, I could not have endured. This book is a distillation of the doodles. If anything in this volume offends you, I apologize in advance and remind you that not only are *some* of my best friends Jewish; virtually *all* of them are, and *most* of them are rabbis (some who do and some who do NOT make house calls). If *nothing* offends you, I will have to improve the book in its second edition, if any. So my qualifications, then, are clear: I have chutzpa!

This book may help you to be Jewish if you want to get on the bandwagon. In any case, it may delight you to

see the warm, amusing, zany side inside Jewish life, as
seen by somebody who loves being Jewish. If not, you're
an anti-Semite even if your topless friends *are* Jewish.

A.V.

I am ___ am not ___ Jewish.
I would like ___ like not ___ to be a sympathetic Jew.
Boy, have you got chutzpa! ___

Contents

xiv

My Rabbi
Doesn't Make
House Calls

1. How to Identify a Jew (*Even If He Doesn't* look *Jewish*)

It is hard to identify a Jew. In the first place, you don't have to be a Jew to be "Jewish." Some Jews are not "Jewish." The late Lenny Bruce, who was Jewish, thought that Italians are "Jewish." (When the Italians formed an Italian Anti-Defamation League, the JEWISH Anti-Defamation League thought the Italians were getting TOO Jewish.) Irishmen who have given up the Church are "Jewish"—and, of course, so were Negroes until recently. So it's not easy to figure out who is Jewish.

Then, of course, the scientists have proven that there is no such thing as a Jewish race. Religion doesn't define Jews, either, because many Jews reject all religious belief. How can you figure a people that includes some parents who name their kids Joshua and Sarah and rear them to be atheists or Unitarians while other parents name their young ones Launcelot and Toni and enroll them in Jewish day schools? So exactly what is the Jewish group? How do you define it? One of the wonderful things about Jews is that we know what we are NOT, but we can't agree on what we ARE. The most controversial issue in Jewish life is: what is a Jew? A Jew has been identified as somebody who goes around asking "What is a Jew?" That controversy stands a better chance than do the Arabs of blowing up the State of Israel.

Anyway, there is no such thing as a Jewish physical type—no Jewish nose, hair, eyes, skin color, height, etc. For proof, one has only to go to Israel and survey the Nordic-looking, blue-eyed blond, snub-nosed young sabras (native-born Israelis); or go to New York City and visit the Black Jews; or trek to Haight-Ashbury in San Francisco to see the many bearded, beaded and barefoot youngsters of doubtful sex but of definite Jewish parentage. Who is Jewish? What is a Jew?

This is a Jewish Neighborhood?

Some people think you can identify a Jew by the neighborhood he lives in. Most Jews live in Jewish neighborhoods. But, even if we knew what a *Jew* is, what is a Jewish *neighborhood*? What percentage of the people are Jewish? Nobody knows. A typical Jewish neighborhood has a Chinese restaurant named Sui Generous, a pizza parlor, a beauty shop, a kosher deli and five synagogues—Reform, Conservative, Orthodox, a split-off from one of the temples, and a split-off from the split-off. The great benefit of living in a Jewish neighborhood is that then you don't have to do anything Jewish. Nobody asks. It's an effortless Jewish life. In small towns, where Gentiles predominate, Jews *must* belong to synagogues. Christian friends ask: "How come your Debby doesn't go to Sunday School?" and "Tell me, what church do you go to?" And the first thing you know, some nice men from the local Christian church raise some money for a site and are out on the lot with hammers and saws to start a fellowship project, building a "church for our Jewish neighbors." For a Jew to refuse to belong *then* is not only to brand himself a fink; it is worse—heresy to the American religion of ecumania (see Chapter 4).

Sometimes, of course, a Christian neighborhood *becomes* a Jewish neighborhood. This happens when an influx of Jews results in an exodus of non-Jews. This pattern has been evident in many suburbs. Some Long Island communities became Jewish almost overnight in the post-World War II era. Some Jews moved in; non-Jews began to move eastward. Then some Jews moved further east on the Island. Non-Jews ran faster. One demographer observed the phenomenon and asked: "When will the non-Jews stop running eastward?" The answer: "Past Montauk, when their hats begin to float."

But the cycle never stops. After the non-Jews flee the Jews, and the neighborhood becomes Jewish, the first Negro families move in, the Jews begin to flee the Negroes, leapfrogging on the heels of the WASPs, who are fleeing both of them, closely followed by the Negroes, who are now moving out of their neighborhood (the Puerto Ricans are coming), which was recently a Jewish neighborhood and just before that had been WASP and *Judenrein*. Where will it all end? Perhaps with integrated hats floating at Montauk.

And yet, incredibly, Jews can usually identify each other. There is a strange subliminal alchemy of intuition, guesswork and sensitivity which leads Jews to be able to locate the *landsman* (fellow Jew). How do they do it?

Locating the Landsman

This Jewish game is played a hundred ways. In reading the newspaper, one's eye automatically flags Jewish-sounding names. If the paper is announcing the Nobel Prize awards, some internal computer notes how many of the winners are Jewish. If thousands of scholarship winners are listed, the eye grows bleary proudly picking out unknown Jewish boys and girls who have earned honors en route to college. If there has been an airplane crash and the paper lists the victims, there is of course a general shudder of horror shared by all readers. For the Jewish reader, there is an additional involuntary sigh for one's ill-fated coreligionists. Or a scandal explodes on page one; the culprits are listed. In a subliminal and anxious flash, any Jewish names are recorded in the mind's eye of the Jewish reader. The brain may even trigger a grimace on the reader's face and bring an audible "oy" to the lips. Why? Perhaps because the Jewish group is so small, its history so tormented and its sense of common destiny so acute.

LTL (Locating the Landsman) is also applied to entertainment—movies, television, literature, sports, theater. Through a magical intelligence system which flashes information faster than Telstar, Jews know that Jerry Lewis, Danny Kaye, Jack Benny, Allie Sherman, Milton Berle, Bess Myerson, Sandy Koufax, Saul Bellow and Sammy Davis, of course, are members of the *mishpachah* (family). Imperialistic Jews tend to be expansionist, stealing across the borders for new conquests. Thus they seek to claim Alec Guinness (his wife is Jewish), Debbie Reynolds (she has been married to two nice Jewish boys—one at a time), Elizabeth Taylor (she used to be Jewish, but she Welshed) and Danny Thomas ("if he's not Jewish, he ought to be"). But this is cheating and, if challenged, calls for surrendering three landsmen you have already successfully located. So one must be careful before making a claim.

To test your own LTL score, check which of the following you believe are Jewish:

Simon and Garfunkel	Allie Sherman	Arthur Burns
Kirk Douglas	Tony Curtis	Henry Kissinger
Groucho Marx	Arthur Goldberg	Sarah Bernhardt
Bernard Malamud	Sigmund Freud	Pierre Mendès-France
Jonas Salk	Dore Schary	Yevgeny Yevtushenko
Disraeli	Lorne Greene	Nicholas Katzenbach
Abe Fortas	Modigliani	John Wayne
Abba Eban	Heinrich Heine	Harlow Shapley
Jacob Javits	Alan Arkin	General Mark Clark
Walter Lippmann	Albert Einstein	Juan Bosch
	Tom Okker	Charlton Heston

The answer is that all except the last seven are (or were) Jewish. Score four points for every correct answer. Ninety to 100 per cent is excellent; 80 to 89 per cent is good; 70 to 79 per cent is embarrassing and means LTL is not your bag. If you scored less than 70 per cent, are you Jewish? You don't *look* Jewish!

LTL can also be played backward, by going back into

history. High points are given for such bona fide claims as this: (a) In the years 1130–1138, Pope Anacletus II was known as a "Jewish Pope" (he was the grandson of a Jewish convert to Catholicism); (b) Columbus had a Jewish navigator named Judah Cresques (known as the "map Jew"); (c) Luis de Torres, Columbus' interpreter, coined the word "turkey," calling the bird *tukki,* Hebrew for peacock; (d) behind George Washington was a Jewish financier, Haym Solomon, who helped make the Revolution possible; (e) Judah Benjamin, Secretary of War of the Confederacy, was Jewish; (f) Jesus was a Jew (technically you get points for this, but it's not worth the argument); (g) Herbert Lehman, former governor (and senator) of New York, and Henry Horner, former governor of Illinois, were Jews. Seven other Jews served as governors, five by election in their own states, two by appointment in territories. Who were they? Play LTL.

In playing LTL, one should be armed with as many historical tidbits such as these as possible. You must throw back four landsmen if you use the same tidbit twice. After all, one should not be a bore in playing LTL. In playing backward, one must also be on special guard not to claim a non-Jew as a landsman. Lately, overzealous Jews have claimed Columbus, the painter Rubens and Pope John. If challenged, such a false claim will cost you ten hard-won landsmen.

Drop the Landsmen

The other side of the LTL coin is DTL (Drop the Landsmen). This game is essential because LTL always turns up a few Jews you don't want, and there must be a way of disposing of them. Who needs to claim Karl Marx, the progenitor of communism; or Jack Ruby, the killer of Oswald; or (remember you can play DTL backward, too, just like LTL) the bloody Jewish King Herod (a Roman Quisling in the first century before the common era)? DTL is the way of disposing of unsavory characters like the above, as well as chronic losers or nudniks (see Chapter 5).

Let's take Karl Marx, for example, to see just how DTL works. You are asked, "Say, was Karl Marx Jewish?" The answer: "No. He was BORN Jewish, yes, but he was baptized in childhood, grew up as a Christian and became an anti-Semite. Besides, he was the prophet of communism and don't you see how badly the communists are treating three million Jews in Russia?" That, of course, is an easy DTL (what with his conversion, etc.). You only gain one good landsman for such an obvious DTL of a bad one.

Let us turn to a stickier case. A man named Matthew Goodman, a vice-president of the local bank, embezzles a half million dollars and runs away and hides in Chile. It is widely believed that he is Jewish, and the surface evidence seems to sustain the finding. You must approach this DTL in a gingerly manner. "Well now, let's just see. Matthew? Matthew? That's not a Jewish name, is it? Did you ever read the New Testament? Matthew was one of Christ's apostles, and his books are not exactly pro-Jewish, I'll tell you. Vice-president of the bank, eh? Are there any Jewish officers in that WASP bank? So why should they make an embezzler vice-president? What do you mean, that's not logical? Besides if he WERE Jewish—

the only Jewish officer in the bank—do you think he would disgrace his people that way? No, he would pause, with his hand in the till, and say: 'Will this be bad for the Jews?' And what is the answer to that question? Obvious! And then he flew away to Chile? Now I ask you: What kind of a place is THAT for a Jewish fellow? If he were Jewish, he'd go to Argentina, nice Jewish community, good delicatessens, hot pastrami, a little Yiddish culture, UJA, Israel Bonds, Jewish theater. Chile? Tin! No, it doesn't figure. How could he spend his money there? Or he would go to Mexico City, probably with a B'nai B'rith pilgrimage. Did you ever see the Jewish Sports Club there? Tennis, swimming, volley ball, golf, dancing, a kosher snack bar—a real mechiah. No, sorry, Goodman cannot be Jewish."

This DTL is definitely worth a pick-up of two good landsmen.

To test your skill at DTL, see how you would dispose of the following:

Jack Ruby	Norman Mailer	Roy Cohn
Ralph Ginzberg	Bernard Goldfine	Mickey Cohen
Walter Winchell	Ilya Ehrenburg	Mark Rudd
Max Baer	Barry Goldwater	Philip Roth

Jewish players of LTL have recently developed delusions of grandeur. It is understandable. With Jewish themes pervading our theater and literature, Yiddish words becoming *de rigueur*, famous personalities converting to Judaism and Jewish foods spicing an entire nation, many Jews have gotten carried away. There are some

Jews who already believe that everybody is Jewish or in the process of becoming so. And, now inevitably, a latent suspicion has framed itself as an ultimate question: Is God Jewish?

2. How to Organize, Avoid and Survive Jewish Meetings

"Well," says the chairman, glancing at his watch, "it is now after eight-thirty [it is really ten to nine, but who is counting?] and the meeting was called for eight. In fairness to those of you who came on time and also to our out-of-town speaker [if it were a *local* speaker we could fiddle around until after nine], I think we should get started." The chairman balefully surveys the small audience scattered among row after row of empty seats [I told them they should set up the smaller room; this speaker is as popular as the German measles] and says: "I am sure that more people will be coming along. However, in looking over the audience, [why do Jews never sit in the first two rows?] I want to assure the distinguished speaker that these people sitting in front of you came here despite the severe competition of other cultural events in town [television] and that, while we may not have quantity, we certainly have quality. The people here assembled represent the leadership of the Jewish community [they should live so long]. And now, with-

out further ado, I would like . . . [I would like to get
the hell out of here by eleven the latest, that's what I'd
like.]" The role of the chairman is to say nothing, and he
does so admirably and at great length.

And so begins another Jewish meeting. Jewish meetings have a ritual, a drama and a flavor all their own.
The constant nature of Jewish meetings is doubtless responsible for the low Jewish birth rate. From the moment
the meeting begins (late) to the moment it ends (late),
after a long hassle as to the time and place of the next
meeting, it is a uniquely and wonderfully Jewish experience. The following are some of the basic rules for
such meetings:

The Out-of-town Speaker

Enthusiasm for the speaker is in direct proportion
to the distance he had to travel. Don't make the fatal
mistake of inviting Dr. Paul Bretman, a genuine authority who happens to live in your own community.
The chairman would introduce him as "our own good
friend and neighbor, Paul," and that would turn everybody off. If he lives in Chicago, Paul is good south of
St. Louis and east of Detroit. That is to say, if your
speaker comes from a hundred miles away or more, he
will qualify as "that distinguished expert." (The imagination boggles at the thousands of out-of-towners
jetting in and out of each other's towns each night in
a mammoth game of flying musical chairs.) Anyway,
you will not invite him back again, which, since he is a
hit-and-run speaker who has one speech and much prefers one night stands, that is fine with him, too. He is

a "Chinese menu speaker": two jokes from A and three clichés from B.

The Introducer with Foot-in-mouth Disease

Pick the introducer with care, either rewarding some-one for a generous gift, setting him up for a future gift, or calming the *macher* (see Chapter 5) whose wife was insulted at the planning committee. (This is known as the Squeaking Wheel Syndrome.) The intro-ducer should, under no circumstances, have the vaguest familiarity with the speaker and his background. He should scramble the pronunciation of the speaker's name (Dr. Robert Druck should come out Rubber Duck and Rabbi Finstein as Rabbit Finster). Of course, he should read every word of the biographical sheet, provided in advance by the speaker, so the audience will not be de-prived of the knowledge of how the speaker skipped the fifth grade in the St. Louis public schools, how his was the first Bar Mitzvah ever celebrated in the Cow Palace in San Francisco and how, during World War ii, he developed a double hernia carrying cases of beer for sailors on Mogmog Island in Ulithi, Pacific. The last line of the introduction should reflect the introducer's own distinctive flourish, as follows:

"I have been assured by those who have heard the speaker before that, when he finishes his address to us, we will be absolutely thrilled. . . ." or

"Of all the ranking dignitaries who have adorned this platform, I believe that our speaker tonight is the rankest. . . ." or

"All of us have heard a great deal about this man

whom we are honored to have address us tonight, so the less said about the speaker the better. . . ." or

"This great man is a speaker beyond recall . . . I mean compare . . . and I give him to you with the greatest of pleasure. . . ." or

"The contributions which this speaker has made can only be described as infinitesimal."

Over-program the Meeting

Start the meeting with an invocation. This not only pays proper obeisance to religion, but permits the rabbi (who knows the out-of-town speaker very well and has the highest contempt for his ability) to give to *God* the speech that he feels *he* should have been invited to present to the *audience*. While he is invoking, the members of the planning committee (who met nine times in one week to prepare for this meeting) will recall how furious the rabbi was when he was asked to pronounce the invocation. ("When will you people learn that a rabbi is something more than a mere invoker and benedictor?") They also know from previous experience how much angrier he would have been if he had not been asked.

After the out-of-town speaker has finished, it is good form to have a panel of five of your own members—a sisterhood lady, a youth, a man from the men's club, a representative of the "big board" and the group's house intellectual (who always says, "This was very *interesting* and *stimulating*, but I think we must ask ourselves several prior questions. Precisely what is our *PURPOSE*, how do we define that *PURPOSE* and how do we propose to achieve that *PURPOSE?*"). While it would be faster and equally useful to have the panel speak simultaneously, there is a higher value in repetition. Long before the panel is done, the audience will have succumbed (being speeched to death is the Jewish form of capital punishment) and the out-of-town speaker will be on a jet winging to Detroit (his plane passing two thousand feet under the plane speeding Paul back from Tulsa). The meeting can then be closed by still another rabbi, who, in his benediction, refutes the main speaker and provides God with a running summary of any points He might have missed in the press of five thousand benedictions being beamed at Him each evening. (God is not really dead; He's just one more victim of over-programing.)

Watch the Logistics

The success or failure of the meeting depends, in no small measure, on the facilities. If it is a banquet, every person should be seated at the four-tier dais so that nobody feels like a second-class citizen.

If, on the other hand, you want to have a conference-type meeting, with give-and-take discussion, have the tables set up either in a T (with the chairman and other machers crossing the T) or in a U (with the ditto at the bottom). Recently, some Jewish organizations have experimented with the double-wing and the I formation. The double-wing has certain advantages (eat on one wing and meet on the other), but it has been found to be too static, and those on the end of the wing tend to fly out the door too easily. The I is excellent if you have two co-chairmen for your club (one on each end of the I) but the people on the vertical line tend to exhaust themselves spinning their heads back and forth like the shuttlecock in the badminton game. The mod procedure is a series of separate tables, which simplifies separate checks and also lends itself to buzz sessions, which is a technique of group dynamics by which small groups are able to evaluate the main address and pose basic questions such as: When is lunch? Who found *that* speaker? What is *Jewish* about our Jewish organization?

Follow the Leader

There are subtle ways to stand out in a crowd, even at a meeting. If you watch closely, you can pick out the natural leader even if he never so much as opens his mouth. He arrives late and breathless and shakes hands all around before settling into a seat next to the chairman. ("Sorry I'm late—the earliest I've been late all year.") Later he will leave early with similar flourishes. In the midst of the proceedings, he will be summoned to a long-distance telephone. ("Is Dr. Jerome Keeler in the room?")

More important, Dr. Keeler will be the very eye of a hurricane of note passing during the meeting. Although he will look completely intent on what the speaker is saying and seem to be taking copious notes on his remarks, he will actually be conducting a rapid-fire simultaneous exchange of notes with at least ten people at the table (one of whom is, of course, positioned at the very opposite end of the room and turns beet red every time one of the messages begins its agonizingly long route around the table).

With diligent research we have pieced together the fragments of notes torn up and shredded after the meetings. (The notes not destroyed are not worth bothering with.) Here are some excerpts: "Man, is this guy a bomb! He's been talking an hour and he hasn't said anything yet." . . . "Boy, this Rappaport is a lousy chairman. How did we ever get stuck with him? Do YOU want to be the next chairman? I can swing it!" . . . "Hey, your eyes are glazing over. Are you asleep already?" . . . "Dear me, I am sending this note to myself, all the way around the table. I'm sick and tired of everybody getting notes except me. I don't have to answer this, but it puts me in the swim." . . . "My organization celebrated its 100th anniversary at a banquet at the Pierre last night, but it didn't get covered by the New York *Times* for some reason, so we're going to have to do it all over again next month." . . . "Who is the wise guy who sent that note about me? If you're planning a coup, forget it. Rappaport" . . . "Listen, I'm cutting out before they start calling cards." . . . "No, I don't want to be chairman. I'd rather have a frontal lobotomy. Let Rappaport have it; he deserves it."

The Space Race

How do you know if your meeting has been successful? By the number of people who attend? No, the Beatles could fill the Rose Bowl, what does it prove? Then by the amount of money raised? No, this is important, but it is not the best criterion. There is only one valid measure: space in the New York *Times* (or the biggest daily paper in your town). If it is not important enough to be noted by the *Times*, it did not happen. If it earns a mere stick—one or two paragraphs—it happened, but barely. If it gains a full column with a by-line, you really made the scene.

Until the New York *Herald Tribune* vanished, Jewish organizations could hedge their bets ("Listen, the *Times* isn't the only paper in town. We can't play favorites. Did you see our story in the *Trib?*"). Now it is do or die with the New York *Times*. To be "skunked" in the *Times* is a form of institutional euthanasia. On the other hand, to win a "Man of the Day" interview or a feature in the Sunday Magazine section is to climb the heights of Jewish institutional glory, unsurpassed, unless it be by the cover of *Time*.

Conventional Wisdom

The climactic Jewish meetings are regional and, especially, national conventions where thousands of delegates gather for an extended period (up to a week) at a big hotel in a large city to advance the work of the organization and of Jewish life. These conventions start an hour early to give delegates time for hugging and kissing. At these conventions the opportunities for overprograming become limitless. Sessions begin with 8 A.M. continental breakfast meetings and continue through forums, workshops, committee meetings, fundraising luncheons, plenaries, caucuses, receptions, banquets and evening programs until 3 A.M., when the resolutions committee begins its work. Large conventions also permit the luxury of hundreds of speakers, even without counting invocations and benedictions. This enhances that sense of personal participation so important to a major organization.

Only a few mammoth hotels throughout the country can accommodate the national conventions of the biggest Jewish organizations. One of these in the Fontainebleau of Miami Beach. This is a favorite hotel for conventions whose themes are poverty and racial integration. It is also very fine for theology and Republicans. Many delegates to a recent convention can still remember the swinging workshop on "The Relevance of Maimonides to Modern Jewish Theology: for the Small Congregation," which was held in the Boom Boom Room of the Fontainebleau. Delegates to this particular hotel now carry maps of the hotel pinned to their lapels; this is to make certain that there is not a recurrence of the regrettable lapse in which eighteen B'nai B'rith delegates got hopelessly lost trying to get from A to F Wing and were baptized at a Southern Baptist workshop on "How Do We Reach Our Jewish Brethren?"

The Resolutionary War

One of the purposes of the convention is to legislate —that is, to make policy for the organization. This is done by the adoption of resolutions. Jewish life could be characterized (but should not be) as still in its *resolutionary* phase. There are several vital rules for the preparation and adoption of resolutions. There are, of course, no rules for the *implementation* of these resolutions. (It is analogous to swatting flies. You don't have to DO anything with the flies once you've swatted them. The fun is in the PROCESS.)

Here are some of the rules:

A. The resolutions should be written in advance by members of the staff. (How do the *delegates* know what resolutions they need?)

B. They should be presented to a resolutions committee, which begins its deliberations at 3 A.M. and meets until the very moment the resolution is presented to the plenary session (so they will be too bleary to do any real damage).

C. The first paragraph of the resolution should quote from Isaiah, thus setting forth the Jewish rationale for the resolution on second-class mailing privileges, air pollution or the tax on Brazilian coffee. (Don't use "Come let us reason together"; it's been done.)

D. The second paragraph should cite "our commitment to those ideals which underlie both our faith and democracy itself," thus lining us up squarely with the free world.

E. The resolution should contain at least twelve whereases and two caveats, thus establishing that we're not shooting from the hip.

F. The last paragraph should constitute a peroration, like "In this way we will advance man and society toward that Kingdom of God, which has been our goal and our vision since the Hebrew prophets first sounded the trumpet call of conscience to all mankind." (This will provide the necessary fat for harmless surgery when the resolution hits the floor. Also, enough layers of fat conceal the heart of the matter.)

And now the resolution is presented to the floor, along with thirty-seven others, by the chairman of the resolutions committee, who begins his report by saying: "It is now five in the afternoon (or, at the latest, five-ten). I know you are all tired, and you will soon want to freshen up for the banquet. If I may have your indulgence, I will read the resolutions seriatim and expeditiously. I do hope you will give us your attention, because my committee and I were up all night and we think these resolutions deserve your careful consideration —for the next forty-five minutes." He then reads the first resolution and moves its adoption.

"Point of information, Mr. Chairman," barks a man at the middle microphone. "I'm Stanley Livstone, at mike number three, from Spokane, Washington. I have only one question: Is there a quorum present?"

The chairman, after hurried whispered consultations with everyone on the dais, explains that, according to the rules of the convention, a quorum consists of 50 per cent of the people present, and "we will now proceed to vote on resolution number one." Mr. Livstone begins to appeal the chair's ruling, but his mike, which is controlled at the dais, goes unaccountably dead.

Mr. Livstone, after running madly from mike to mike looking for a live one, surrenders by the time the assembly gets up to resolution number ten (on anti-Semitic scrawling on subway ads) and gives up to go upstairs to freshen up. One by one, the other delegates shuffle out. The floor is emptying. As the exodus increases, the chairman hits the panic button and reads faster, determined to hit the finish line before the stenotypist and the parliamentarian also depart. As the buzz of the departing delegates rises, the chairman tears through the resolutions in staccato barks like a tobacco auctioneer. Enough with the seriatim: "I have here a resolution on better service to chapters. It's *for* it. Do I hear a second? Good. Do I hear any objection? It is so ordered. I have here a resolution on the perpetuation of the Jewish people. We're for it. Second? Objection? So ordered. I have here a resolution on communism. We're against it. . . . etc., etc."

And so the report of the resolutions committee is adopted, and the course of the organization is charted for the next year. Before pounding the gavel for adjournment, the chairman turns to his associates, now comatose at the front table (there are no more delegates in the hall), and declaims: "I cannot refrain from expressing my deep gratitude to you and myself for demonstrating once again that we, the delegates, set policy in this organization in the best deliberative tradition of American democracy. We stand adjourned!"

Veterans of Jewish conventions, except for those who develop hernias from carrying the delegate's kit, have long since learned how to sleep with their eyes wide open, a look of eager earnestness fixed upon their faces. Such an old pro rarely falls off his chair in the middle of a plenary session. The hardest-working delegates are, by all odds, the rabbis. They invariably carry a notebook and record every good idea—or joke, especially jokes—they hear. Said one of the finest American rabbis, "When

I listen to so many good sermon ideas, I practically get laryngitis." A superior convention can fill the average rabbi with a median payload of ten sermons. If there are two or three rabbis present from the same congregation, there may be the pulling of rank or the drawing of either straws or swords.

Appoint a Committee

This is the ultimate denouement, which justifies all that precedes. Jewish life without committees would be like lox without bagels or like a men's club breakfast without a comedian. Jewish life is not exactly a movement; it's a series of ad hoc committees.

A committee is a process of collective masochism. It is easy to ridicule, difficult to endure and harder to leave than flypaper. It is a bromide that a camel is a horse put together by a committee. It is also said that when Lindbergh was asked how he was able to fly the Atlantic, he said: "Because I didn't have to fly with a committee." Lindbergh was not Jewish. That should give one pause.

If Moses had had a committee, the Ten Commandments would now be a draft document marked "Not for Publication," being "processed" by an editorial committee for "language" and subject to the veto of the separate boards of each tribe. The prophets could never have gotten their wild preachments through any committee. "Beat your swords into plowshares" would have come out of the wringer of the Prophetic Advisory Committee something like "wherever practicable, subject to national security and on an ad hoc basis only, earnest

consideration should be given to the feasibility and de-
sirability of converting swords, etc. . . ."

Jews are unusually subject to committees. Nobody
knows why. Perhaps for the same reason they are subject to ulcers. One of the most interesting types of
committee is the *co-ordinating* committee, consisting of
representatives from several organizations. Most representatives come to the meetings in order to check up on
what the other organizations are doing, and to eat lunch.
Co-ordinators are a very special breed of cat; their slogan is "Deputize, organize, supervise—but, for heaven's
sake, don't *work!*" If the co-ordinating agency *works*,
that is called *functioning* and it is regarded as a foul
blow, like serving ham.

Co-ordinators prepare agendas, call meetings, keep
minutes, pass out sandwiches and seltzer, walk on eggs,
play it by ear, get down to the nitty-gritty, whisper
the correct names to the chairman, invest trivia with an
aura of importance, circulate pink confidential memo-
randa in advance of the meeting (marked "Destroy before reading") and try to keep the members of the
committee from breaking up on the shoals of "philosophic differences," which, freely translated, means
"*credit.*" Votes are rarely taken. Things are decided on
"the sense of the meeting," which means the chairman
does what he and the co-ordinator think best when
everybody else goes home. Co-ordinating committees are
powerful brakes against irresponsible action. This is
achieved by the simple device of discouraging any action
whatsoever. In extreme circumstances, where action

erupts in spite of this careful process, it is time to hire a co-ordinator to co-ordinate the co-ordinators.

To get the most out of a Jewish meeting, whether large or small, it is imperative to understand the vocabulary. The following is a glossary of frequently used terms and their real meanings:

3. How to Understand the Scene at Jewish Meetings: A Glossary*

WE OBJECT TO THE MANNER IN WHICH THIS MOTION HAS BEEN RAILROADED THROUGH. We had arranged for my side to put in our motion first.

I AM SURE THAT MR. BERG HAS EXCELLENT AUTHORITY TO BACK HIS CONCLUSION. He doesn't know what he's talking about.

I DON'T QUESTION THE SINCERITY OF MR. STEIN'S STATEMENT. I question the sincerity of Mr. Stein's statement.

MR. GLASER IS A MOST DEVOTED AND TIRELESS MEMBER OF OUR BOARD. Mr. Glaser is a NUDNIK.

I DON'T THINK WE SHOULD WASTE TIME GOING OVER THE MINUTES OF OUR LAST MEETING. Miss Klotznick never typed them.

* This glossary appeared originally in the pages of *American Judaism* and is reprinted with permission. The glossary was compiled jointly by Mr. Paul Kresh, editor of *American Judaism,* and Albert Vorspan.

WOULD YOU RESTATE THE MOTION? They're not going to put anything over on me.

I HAD SOME REMARKS PREPARED FOR ME BY THE STAFF, BUT I FEEL SO CLOSE TO THIS GROUP I WOULD RATHER JUST SPEAK FROM MY HEART. I will now make the remarks prepared for me.

MY WORTHY COLLEAGUE . . . My worst enemy should have such a colleague.

I DON'T THINK WE CAN TAKE RESPONSIBILITY FOR THE BEHAVIOR OF EVERY INDIVIDUAL JEW. A Jewish gonif is on the front pages.

I THINK THE ENTIRE JEWISH COMMUNITY CAN TAKE PRIDE IN THE ACHIEVEMENTS OF THIS GREAT AMERICAN. Arthur Goldberg has been named to a new post.

I THINK WE MUST BEAR IN MIND THE PUBLIC RELATIONS IMPLICATIONS OF SUCH A MOVE. The goyim won't like it.

ARE THERE ANY FURTHER NOMINATIONS? It's all settled.

I'M JUST TALKING OFF THE TOP OF MY HEAD. I don't know what I'm talking about.

I DON'T RECALL THE EARLIER COMMENT, BUT I DO BELIEVE . . . I just woke up.

LET'S SET UP A PILOT PROJECT. Let's kill it for a year.

I MISSED PART OF THE MEETING, BUT WHAT I HEARD WAS MOST STIMULATING. After I made my own comment, I fell asleep.

LET'S ADOPT THE IDEA IN PRINCIPLE AND HAVE THE EXACT LANGUAGE WORKED OUT LATER. Let's kill this crazy idea and go home already.

LET'S GET DOWN TO TACHLIS. 1. Let's change the subject. 2. Let's avoid a decision at all costs.

WHY DON'T WE LEAVE THESE DETAILS TO BE WORKED OUT BY THE STAFF. It's not important anyway.

THE STATEMENT IS WONDERFULLY STRONG, BUT I THINK THE COMMITTEE SHOULD GO OVER IT. It's too strong.

WOULD THE WAITERS PLEASE CLEAR THE HALL? Here comes the pitch.

THE PREVIOUS SPEAKER HAS ALREADY SAID MUCH OF WHAT I HAD IN MIND, BUT IT BEARS REPEATING. He stole the only idea I had.

ALLOW ME THESE FEW MOMENTS . . . consider the evening shot.

I WILL CONFINE MYSELF TO A FEW BRIEF RE-MARKS. We'll be lucky to get home for the Late, Late Show.

I'VE GIVEN THIS MUCH THOUGHT. On the way up in the elevator.

WILL YOU WITHHOLD YOUR APPLAUSE UNTIL
I HAVE INTRODUCED ALL THE PEOPLE ON THE
DAIS? Everybody's on the dais.

JEWISH LIFE IS AT THE CROSSROADS. There's a
new emergency—on top of the usual crises and catastrophes.

THE RESOLUTIONS COMMITTEE MEETS IN PARLOR C. The resolutions committee meets in Parlor E—
in the other wing of the hotel.

I'M GLAD TO SEE THE YOUTH HERE, BECAUSE
THEY ARE THE LEADERS OF TOMORROW. Who
let all those kids in?

A TOKEN OF OUR APPRECIATION FOR HIS MANY
YEARS OF UNSTINTING AND DEDICATED DE-
VOTION TO CIVIC AND JEWISH CAUSES . . . Another plaque.

WE HAVE JUST SENT A TELEGRAM TO THE
STATE DEPARTMENT. We ran out of stationery.

SPEAKING FOR MYSELF, I'M VERY GLAD YOU
BROUGHT THAT QUESTION UP. I was afraid some
joker would bring that up.

EVERYBODY WHO KNOWS ME KNOWS THAT I
STRONGLY BELIEVE JEWS SHOULD STAND UP
AND BE COUNTED. Except in this case.

WE ALL ADMIRE MR. FERGASSON AS A DISTIN-
GUISHED JEWISH COMMUNAL, CIVIC AND PHIL-
ANTHROPIC LEADER. He's a big giver.

WE THANK HERB FOR HIS MOST DETAILED AND THOROUGH REPORT. HE HAS CERTAINLY GIVEN US FOOD FOR THOUGHT. Let's eat.

MIND YOU, I HAVE NO OBJECTION TO THE PRINCIPLE OF THIS PROJECT, BUT I SIMPLY THINK WE SHOULD CAREFULLY EXAMINE ALL THE IMPLICATIONS OF IT. I'm against it.

OUR COMMITTEE HAS PROCEEDED SLOWLY AND CAUTIOUSLY. We haven't had a meeting yet.

I WONDER IF WE COULD RETURN TO THIS POINT A LITTLE LATER. Let's bury it.

I'D LIKE MR. BERG TO HEAR THIS. Berg, stop talking and listen!

THIS IS SUCH AN IMPORTANT SUGGESTION AND THE HOUR IS SO LATE, WHY CAN'T WE PUT THIS OVER TO ANOTHER MEETING WHEN OUR MINDS ARE FRESH? Let's kill this dopey idea and go home.

I MUST SAY YOU HAVE ASKED A VERY SEARCHING AND CHALLENGING QUESTION. I wish I knew the answer.

NOBODY FEELS MORE STRONGLY THAN I DO THAT JEWS MUST BE IN THE FOREFRONT OF SOCIAL JUSTICE. Let's stay out of it.

OUR DECISION TO POOL OUR EFFORTS WITH THOSE OF ALL THE OTHER SYNAGOGUES IN THE COMMUNITY IN DEVELOPING A JOINT

COMMUNITY-WIDE PROGRAM REFLECTS OUR DEEP COMMITMENT TO KLAL YISROEL, TO THE PEOPLEHOOD OF ISRAEL. This way we can split the costs.

I'M GLAD YOU BROUGHT THAT UP. You should only drop dead.

WE HAVE PUBLISHED THE BEST AVAILABLE TEXT. A lousy book.

4. How to Be an Ecumaniac

Ecumenism has made the scene with Jews, as with all other religious groups. Cardinal Cushing has, by now, spoken in practically every synagogue in Boston. Priests, nuns and monks march with rabbis and ministers all over the place. No public event can get started without a priest, minister and rabbi offering up their joint blessings. Howard Johnson's restaurants provide cards with blessings over the meal for four faiths (Greek Orthodox is the late starter). Ecumenism is coming at us by land and by sea. For example, Port Washington, Long Island, is blessed with three—count them—separate yacht clubs: the Knickerbocker, mostly Jewish; the Manhasset Bay Club, mostly Protestant; and the Port Washington Club, mostly Roman Catholic. The interreligious boating traffic got so bad during weekend races that all three clubs got together to form an umbrella outfit called Cow Bay Racing Association, thus assuring watery ecumaniacal amity.

People who never before had the time of day for each

other are now turned on by dialogue about the nature of God and the condition of man. Judaism, Protestantism and Catholicism are involved together in a host of social causes. It is, decidedly, a new day.

It was not always thus. Only a few years ago, interfaith was essentially a Jewish play looking for Christian actors. Jews invented the interfaith movement and it then lacked only one thing: Christians. Jewish inspiration and money created the Brotherhood Week phenomenon, in which non-Jews were attracted by a lavish banquet and a guilty conscience to enjoy brotherhood with Jews. Spokesmen for each group spoke of their love for each other and how alike they really all were and then went home and didn't see each other again for another year. Psychologists wondered out loud whether an uninhibited HATE WEEK might not be psychologically healthier and more conducive to sound interfaith relations than the hypocritical charade of Brotherhood Week.

In those early days, if a typical interfaith rally in a community attracted a hundred persons, the breakdown would be something like this: ninety-three Jews; four little old ladies of both sexes who attended all meetings; and three interfaithers. Protestants were not quite so difficult to dragoon as Catholics. Only a Jewish Don Quixote would then expect to gain a Catholic priest, perhaps the most inaccessible person in American life in those days of separate but equal religious ghettoes. And if the sisterhood did not tempt the community with a "collation," even the interfaithers would not show.

Now this is all changed. The new spirit of ecumenicism, coming out of Rome and pulsing through American religious life, has ushered in an era of refreshing communication and co-operation. For a church or temple to undertake something alone now virtually exposes it to charges of parochialism. Going it alone is the new religious heresy. For most Jews this new spirit seemed almost millennial. Sitting down with Christians suddenly turned out to be much easier and more interesting than sitting down with other Jews. Then the problems began.

The Religious Dialogue

What could be nicer than having a dialogue between some of the laymen of the temple and the nearby church? Long overdue. The first meeting is arranged. Everybody wears his interfaith smile. But what should we dialogue about? One of the Episcopalians suggests let's talk about God. One of the Jewish laymen says, of course, but he thinks to himself: "My God, *what* God? *Your* God or *my* God?" One of the Jews suggests, let's talk about something concrete, maybe human relations in our community. One of the Episcopalians says that would be nice but he thinks to himself: "Oh, oh, they want to talk about our exclusive Foxhunt Country Club, *that's* what this is all about." One of the Christians says: "Say, I have an idea. Let's talk about our respective prayer books." One of the Jews replies: "Good idea." He thinks to himself: "A hell of a subject. I don't know any more about *ours* than I do about *his*." Another Jew says: "I don't think we should pussyfoot around and we ought to be frank and talk about our differing attitudes toward Jesus." One of his fellow Jews mutters to himself: "Shlemeil, you want them to try to *convert* you at the very first session?" And one of the Christians growls to himself: "Here it comes; they're going to *kill* Him *again.*" The dialogue finally gets started. The subject: Brotherhood.

Such dialogues often prove that when a Jew who does not really believe in Judaism meets a Christian who does not really believe in Christianity, they find they have much in common. They also sometimes prove that a good Jew among goyim is often a goy among Jews just as a good Christian among Jews is often regarded as a neuter among Christians.

The Youth

Could anything be more natural and appropriate than bringing the fresh air of interfaith friendships to our youngsters in the church and synagogue? Nothing indeed. But don't do it. Oompossible. Everybody is for interreligious contacts for the youngsters, especially the youngsters themselves, except for one important group: their parents. Parents want their children to appreciate other religious groups, but in the abstract, not the flesh. Interfaith meetings for the youth are acceptable so long as the kids are eight years old or younger. Anything beyond that—and the nearer to the brink of puberty, the more menacing—is trouble. Intermarriage is on the rise among Jews, especially in small towns, where Jewish youngsters think marrying a Jewish mate is practically incest. You want to have an interreligious discussion among teenagers? Good, especially if the topic is black anti-semitism, dope, or interfaith dating. But how do you know that the discussion will not lead to dance, and dance to date, and date to dalliance and dalliance to mixed marriage? The solution is very simple. Forget it. Interfaith, like youth, is too good to waste on young people.

Time

Ecumenism has become altogether too wearing. One Protestant minister in the Midwest, serving on seventeen interfaith committees in the community, put two private phones in his office—one for the rabbi, one for the priest (his parishioners can reach him only by mail). A rabbi in Maryland, who is secretly bored to tears by the Methodist minister with whom he spends hours every day, waxed nostalgic about the good old days when the Christians would have nothing to do with him. A priest in New England is said to have become so fat on Jewish cooking that he couldn't get into his own confessional. Interfaith is fast becoming a new ministry, in which the peripatetic clergyman has little time and energy left over for the congregation that pays his salary.

The Vanishing WASP

Ecumaniacs worry about prejudice and discrimination against Jews, Catholics, Negroes, Indians, Mexican-Americans, Puerto Ricans and many other minorities. But they never worry about the forgotten victims of discrimination in America: WASPs. The situation in Hollywood illustrates the problem. The film makers decide to make a movie out of a sleazy novel about an Italian mobster. In the laundering process of rendering the book into a movie, the Italian Catholic is transformed into a white Anglo-Saxon Protestant named Smith. Who wants to antagonize two minorities, especially one now guarded by the trigger-happy Italian-American Anti-Defamation League? The same goes for unsavory bigots who happen to be Jewish, Catholic, Negro, Mexican, Chinese, Indian, Mormon. Community relations means don't touch it with a ten-foot pole, for each group has a fervent pressure committee *and* a mimeograph machine.

But who looks out for the neglected white Anglo-Saxon Protestants (who have nothing but the Executive Suite and the Establishment to their names)? Nobody. The result is that only a white Anglo-Saxon can emerge on film as a sonofabitch. (You can, of course, make him a Scot; only Scots seem to *enjoy* ethnic slurs against themselves.) But are Jews, Mexicans, Negroes, Indians, etc., always the victims of bigotry and never the culprits? Are only WASPs anti-Semites and racists? Are racial and religious minority members always pure? The time has come for drastic action. As Jews more and more become WASHes (White Anglo-Saxon Hebrew), and every minority organizes its own pressure group to monitor films and television, it is time to organize a new sock-it-to-'em "Committee for Fair and Equal Allocation of Sonsabitches Among All Minorities." There is no time to lose, because white Anglo-Saxon Protestants in any event will soon be an extinct breed (down to 3 per cent in New York City) in our larger cities. Ecumaniacs should promptly give them a measure of dignity before they disappear altogether.

Ecumenism is making its mark in politics, too, but it's

not all good. I. F. Stone said in 1968: "If the race that produced Isaiah is down to Goldwater, and the race that produced Pericles is down to Agnew, the time has come to give the country back to the WASPS."

We may be on the threshold of a new breakthrough: internal ecumania. As Fletcher Knebel pointed out in an article on "THE WASPS: 1968" in *Look* Magazine (July 23, 1968): "The prospect of economic siege is not all that agitates the WASP. He finds new cause for alarm in Dr. Christiaan Barnard's heart transplants. For, if a mulatto heart can be snugly anchored beneath a white chest, might not the day arrive when an aging proper Bostonian would lunch at his Somerset Club with a Negro kidney, a Jewish left auricle, a Catholic liver, 12 feet of healthy intestine donated by an American Indian and a cornea from the eye of a Japanese-American airline stewardess? And what would the late George Apley say to that?" The man of the future may be a walking ecumaniac with a Jewish heart.

The Ecumenical Crunch

Ecumenism is an idea whose time has come, but don't think the Messiah has arrived. America's melting pot still doesn't melt; it mostly just lies there. Recently, a beer company ran a series of superb ethnic commercials, showing the folk culture of each group in a warm and positive setting as each group enjoyed that brand of beer. The theme was "We must be doing something right." Wrong. Depth research revealed that the ads boomeranged. Why? Members of each group lost interest in a beer that the *other* minorities enjoyed.

Ecumania is a fair-weather sport. It goes smoothly
when all is quiet on the interreligious front. It goes to
pieces in a crunch. Let the Arabs and Israelis have a
go at each other again, and the amiable dialogues in
America become angry cockpits overnight. Let Pope
Paul bomb birth control and the acrimony bubbles. "The
Pope should loop before he leaps," some interfaithers
(mainly Catholic) murmur. Or let blacks and Jews fight
and the white Christian inter-faithers will gladly hold
their coats.

Intra-Jewish Ecumenism

There is still another problem with Jewish ecumania.
What if Jews learn to get along with Catholics? And with
all Protestant denominations, ranging from High Church
Episcopalians and even hitting below the Bible Belt
fundamentalists? Will the various Jewish groups compete with each other for the right to interfaith with the
Christians? Indeed they will! Recently there was a dinner in New York at which the heads of the Reform, Conservative and Orthodox seminaries addressed an intra-
religious gathering of Jews. It was an historic occasion
but, outside the hotel, ultra-Orthodox pickets denounced
the Orthodox speaker for the crime of acknowledging
the legitimacy of Reform and Conservative Judaism.
Work with Christians, *si!* With one's fellow Jews? Let's
not get carried away.

Far from rushing into their own council of *aggiorna-
mento,* Jewish organizations are eyeing each other with
perhaps heightened suspicion in the era of ecumenism.
Someday soon there may be a Christian-Jewish dialogue
planned somewhere, and participants will have to cross

a picket line replete with a bevy of Jewish signs proclaiming: "The Methodists are ours; why don't you stay with the Lutherans?"—"We saw them first"—"We are certified by the Council of Churches."

One of the cardinal guides to Jewish action is *ma yomru ha-goyim*, which means, simply, what will the Gentiles say? If the rabbi wants his members to join in a freedom march, he can summon the prophets, invoke the sublime teachings of the Torah and quote the flaming injunctions of the sages. *Gornisht helfen*. It won't help. But if he says that our neighboring Catholics and Protestants are marching and how will it look if we don't, his people are sure to get with it. This is known as ecumenical social action.

There are some rabbis who despise the idea of ma yomru ha-goyim. They insist it is a sycophantic and servile subservience to public relations. Our guide should not be good relations at all costs, but God's way at any cost, they say. What would the prophets have done? A few of these rabbis have learned ruefully that if they want to be prophets, they'd better live in the desert, because their synagogues are non-prophet institutions. Some of these rabbis go in for pastoral counseling, put a couch and no chairs in their offices and spend the rest of their careers massaging the egos of their congregants and looking down their noses at the social actioniks!

The Rules of the Game

Everybody knows that the best kind of ecumenical co-operation is action, not talk. An ecumenical committee is the forum which permits endless talk about the importance of action. There is something unique about an ecumenical committee. For one thing, the food is less edible than when any one group meets separately. What with the various religious taboos, real and imagined, it always boils down to tuna salad and damp potato chips served by the ladies auxiliary. Then there is the new language of ecumania. One isn't fed up to the teeth; one "has a concern." One doesn't just throw an issue on the table; he "lifts it up for consideration." One doesn't just talk; he "addresses himself" to something. In addition, there is the perennial problem of equal time. If a Catholic priest, through some oversight, invokes the group two meetings in a row, batten down the hatches. If the group meets in a Protestant church three meetings running, it may trigger a Kulturkampf.

Also, there is the Parkinson's Law of Ecumenical Relations: the more ecumenical the venture, the greater the publicity and the less the action. The Parkinson's Law is expressed: $E=P-A$, $E(\text{Ecumania})=P(\text{Publicity})-A(\text{Action})$. The reason you should not look for action here is not any lack of good will. On the contrary, good will brims so full that the interfaith cup often runneth over. The hang-up is: 1) any sharp idea must have its edges softened so it doesn't cut the sensibilities of any of the faith groups; 2) thereafter, what's left of the common denominator idea must be "taken back" to the constituent bodies for approval. This process is sometimes lengthy. If the Catholic Church had been able to speed up this process, there might not have been any Protestant Reformation. Similarly, there are descendants of the original Colonists who are still patiently waiting

for King George of England to get back to them on our
original demands. The mills of the gods grind slowly;
the wheels of ecumenism spin through all eternity.

Reality

Despite all the dramatic changes in the upper eche-
lons of the interfaith scene, ordinary Christians and
Jews still don't know each other very well. When the
dialogue sessions end, each group slips back to its
separate ghetto under cover of the 5 o'clock shadow.
Jews tend by choice to live in Jewish neighborhoods, especially in suburbia; Catholics and Protestants similarly
have their own neighborhoods. And, notwithstanding all
the interfaithing of recent years, most people seem to
like it that way. One result of the interfaith spirit is that
members of each group, without in any way surrendering their deep-seated ambivalence about the others, now
feel somewhat guilty about the self-segregation they have
chosen and really enjoy. So they play games with themselves and with each other about the ecumenical lives
they think they should be living.

So you want to be a Jewish ecumaniac? To play Let's
Be Ecumaniac, Jewish readers can fill out the following
questionnaire:

Is your lawyer non-Jewish?	Yes___	No___
Is your shrink non-Jewish?	Yes___	No___
Is your accountant non-Jewish?	Yes___	No___
Is your best friend non-Jewish?	Yes___	No___
Is your next-door neighbor non-Jewish?	Yes___	No___

Have you had dinner in a non-Jewish
home in the past six months?   Yes__ No__
Would you like to live in a neighborhood
less Jewish than your present one?   Yes__ No__
Is your left auricle non-Jewish?   Yes__ No__
Have you visited the church nearest you? Yes__ No__
Have you read the New Testament? (We
didn't ask you about the Old Testament.) Yes__ No__

Score one point for each YES answer. If you score ten,
you are a liar. If you score seven to nine, you are a true-
blue ecumaniac. A score of six means you've got some
kind of a psychological hang-up. If between two and
five, you're basically a ghetto Jew and you love it. If you
answered every question with a question, your Jewish
instincts are unsullied. If zero or one is your total, you
are anti-Christian and should report to the nearest office
of the National Conference of Christians and Jews for
the cure.

5. How to Get Gray at the Temple (*Or Bald in the Center*)

The Care and Feeding of the Rabbi

The unquestioned leader of the Jewish community is the rabbi. He is, at one and the same time, preacher, ambassador to the Gentiles, teacher, fund-raiser, pastoral counselor, administrator and executive of the Establishment. In some congregations, engaged in building programs, he may also be auxiliary architect, artist and contractor as well. The rabbi is the *kolbo-nik*, master of all trades and man for all seasons. Subjected to impossible and conflicting pressures upon his time and energy, including a host of tasks for which he was not prepared at the rabbinic seminary, he renders a remarkable service to the Jewish and general community. His prestige is high, although he knows better than anyone else how few of his people actually follow his lead. While agonizingly aware in his secret heart that most of his congregants have merely given him their proxy insofar as prayer and Jewish learning are concerned, he refuses to give up the ceaseless effort to lift the level of Jewish commitment and belief.

There are several varieties of rabbis—Reform, Conservative and Orthodox. The Conservative congregation is usually called a center; the Reform synagogue is usually called a temple. Thus it is that Conservative rabbis get bald at the center and Reform rabbis get gray in the temple. But all rabbis have one hair-raising experience in common: the Pulpit Committee.

The pulpit committee combines the best traits of the African headhunt, the Spanish Inquisition and the American political convention. It is the very worst way to pick a rabbi, except for all other ways. But inherent in it are vagaries both subtle and severe, as can be seen from the following purely fictional chronicle of one of the favorite indoor games of American Jews:

Temple Ohev Tsores, the largest congregation in Yeckville, has just lost its rabbi, who, unknown to the congregation, had had his name placed on a "panel" from the Rabbinical Placement Committee and, after rejections by thirteen other congregations, had just made a happy marriage with Temple Sholom (which is Hebrew for "peace" and is the invariable name taken by a temple after a tumultuous split-off from another temple). There was much wailing, weeping and gnashing of teeth among the leadership of Congregation Ohev Tsores, the sharp fact of their own rabbi's defection causing them to forget that many of them had devoted their best energies for seven years past to getting rid of him. Indeed, one of the officers, who had waged a non-stop guerrilla war against him on the grounds that he was too political

("What does a minimum wage have to do with religion?"), now insisted that the rabbi had no right to leave and threatened to take the matter to the Rabbinic Conference Ethics Committee.

No matter; the die was cast. Rabbi Bodek was definitely leaving and already a new-born charisma of warmth and spirituality was retrospectively thrust upon him. ("Let's face it, we'll never have another rabbi like Bodek.") The future had to be attended to. A pulpit committee was named, the chairmanship was naturally given to the man who had said, "Two will get you five you come up with a zombie," and the most intense search outside of Scotland Yard was on.

What kind of rabbi do we want? pondered the committee. Young or old? Hot or cool on social action? Big or small on pastoral counseling? Handsome or not too good-looking? It was never settled, but the consensus was that he should be married; neither too young nor too old (forty is too old); a good preacher, but for no more than twenty minutes; a good mixer; a regular fellow (he should be able to listen to an off-color joke, but not tell one); a hard worker; a challenge to the congregation, but not a nudnik; an effective teacher (mostly for the kids); and a fine representative to the Christians. In short, he should be exactly like the rabbi now departing, who had never been so cherished in the flesh as he was now being venerated in nostalgia.

And now they come, one by one, the candidates. Although they couldn't be more diverse physically, they sound remarkably alike ("I will insist on raising the standards of the religious school. . . . Adults must learn.

. . . Judaism is not a juvenile religion, you know. . . .
I can't visit you unless I know you're sick. . . . My pulpit will be a free pulpit. . . . I can't do it alone. . . .
Judaism has to be relevant to modern life; it's not a
shrine for a dead past.").

The questions start slow, but are soon being pitched
vigorously (50 per cent curves, 25 per cent bean balls)
and the rabbi, depending on his individual skill and
previous experience with the banalities of pulpit committees, either takes the pitch, knocks it out of the park,
goes down swinging, or bunts.

"Tell me, Rabbi, do you consider yourself a Zionist?"
(Answer: "Well, I no longer know what a Zionist is.
Now that there is a state of Israel, etc.")

"Do you think the rabbi or the board should lead?"
("Partnership, etc.")

"Would you object to the temple bowling league?"
("As a person, no, but I have doubts about the Jewish
significance of bowling.")

"We are considering bingo in the temple. What would
be your feeling about that?" ("I, personally, don't think
gambling belongs in the temple, but . . .")

"Should Hebrew play an important role in the school?"
("I feel that Hebrew is important. However . . .")

"Do you speak on political issues?" ("Well now, what
do you mean by 'political?'")

"What would you do to stimulate attendance at services?" ("See to it that leaders like you attend regularly.")
Murmur of discontent.

"I hope this isn't indelicate, but what about your
wife? Will she play an active role in the Sisterhood,

for example? And, by the way, do you happen to have a snapshot of your wife in your wallet?" ("I mean, are you looking for a rabbi or hiring a couple? Hope you folks are not expressing *wife backlash,* you should pardon the pun.")

Finally, months later, the course is run; the rabbis most desired prove unavailable or no longer interested, and the choice comes down to Rabbi Parveh, who neither offended nor excited a single member of the pulpit committee. In presenting him to the congregation for the first time, the president says: "And you can be assured we combed the country from East to West to find the man best suited to fill this pulpit, so capably held for seven years by our beloved Rabbi Bodek. There was never any doubt in the Pulpit Committee that Rabbi Parveh was the spiritual leader we were looking for. He is our unanimous and enthusiastic selection and we present him with our prayerful gratitude to the committee for a hard job brilliantly done."

And, remarkably, Rabbi Parveh turned out to be a first-rate rabbi, despite occasional needling and sniping from a small group of malcontents, almost all of whom, of course, had been members of the pulpit committee.

Whack the Rabbi

Whack the Rabbi is the Jewish equivalent of shooting fish in a barrel. It is a game played in every synagogue of every branch of Judaism. Usually it is harmless; sometimes it is vicious. WHY it is played universally is an interesting psychological mystery. No doubt it has something to do with the guilt feelings Jews must harbor for having made the rabbi their religious surrogate. Perhaps it is secret envy at the prestige and status which attaches to the very title "Rabbi." Perhaps it reflects the secularist spirit regnant in Jewish life. Maybe it is a latent anti-rabbinism which has roots in earlier generations. Maybe it's sublimation—we can't hit our kids but, oh, the rabbi! Whatever it is, Jews seem to delight in the game of Whack the Rabbi.

Rules of the game:

Any number can play. Players are usually (but not always) members of a synagogue. It is not considered good form to Whack the Rabbi of another institution; that is POACHING. It is regarded as bad sportsmanship to Whack the Rabbi during the first three months (the honeymoon) or the last three months of his tenure (lame duck). Anytime between these two periods is appropriate.

Here are some examples of whacks:

The rabbi greets you warmly on the reception line after Sabbath services: "Good *Shabbes*, nice to see you." You respond with an inside double whack: "Glad to see you, too, rabbi. I would also like to have seen you when I was home with a broken leg, but you never came to visit me. Wassamatter, rabbi, you don't make house calls? I mean, after all, I *am* one of your rare admirers."

The rabbi takes a strong public position against a pot bust at the local college. It is carried on page one of the local newspaper under the headline: "Rabbi Says Get off the Pot!" This affords you a great opportunity to deliver a public whack, which, among those who play the game best, is regarded as twice as valuable as an inside whack. You write a letter to the newspaper: *"The Rabbi Does Not Speak for Me!"*

The temple board is locking horns in controversy about the new building plan. The rabbi expresses his opinion. You can, if you are not alert, pass the rabbi's comments by. But, if you are quick, you can slip in an effective whack: "WITH ALL DUE DEFERENCE, RABBI, I THINK THIS IS A *BUSINESS* MATTER FOR US *BUSINESSMEN* TO SOLVE!" . . . and then you can proceed, without jurisdictional confusion, to bankrupt the temple.

The rabbi makes a plea from the pulpit for more generous U.S. foreign aid. You greet the rabbi in the receiving line: "Rabbi, tell me. What is your experience in international economics and geopolitics?" And before the rabbi can respond, you cross with a whack to the jaw: "And when are you going to stop preaching about social justice and start talking about Torah?"

The rabbi is confined to a hospital bed after an appendectomy and the president of the congregation visits him and announces beamingly that he brings the best wishes of the Board of Trustees as expressed in a resolution adopted just last night by a vote of seventeen to four.

"Rabbi," says the president of the youth group, "I LOVED BEING AT CAMP THIS SUMMER. Really turned me on! THOSE RABBIS, THEY ARE REAL SWINGERS, RUNNING AROUND IN THEIR BERMUDAS, STRUMMING GUITARS AND SINGING SONGS UNTIL THE MIDDLE OF THE NIGHT. (Pause) YOU'VE NEVER BEEN TO CAMP, HAVE YOU, RABBI?"

"Rabbi," says the disgruntled chairman of the Social Action Committee, "do you carry a picture of your Board of Trustees in your wallet?"

Crack the Whack

No rabbi worth his salt will take his WHACKS lying down. Veteran rabbis develop psychological armor and strong defenses. Getting their whacks is a toughening experience. Coping with whacks, and cracking them, is a challenge to a rabbi's self-respect and survival. While whacks are par for the rabbinic course, they can become too much to bear during the open season on rabbis (six months before contract renewal). If all else fails, however, the rabbi can issue a flaming statement in behalf of civil rights or against Christian silence, tell the press that the congregation cravenly attempted to muzzle the voice of prophetic Judaism and leave town in a blaze of glory, a martyr to social justice, undeterred by a bunch of small-minded reactionaries. This is an ultimate Crack the Whack and it can hardly fail to win the attention of the pulpit committee of a larger congregation somewhere else.

Games Rabbis Play

Rabbis can fully relax only with each other. Just as Jews generally are most comfortable with their fellow Jews because only with *them* does one NOT have to feel like a Jew ("I'm less comfortable with non-Jews because I think they think of you as a Jew. Jews don't really think of you as a Jew."), rabbis can only cease being rabbis when they are with their fellow rabbis. In small groups, that is; rabbinical conventions are another story.

Only with a colleague, over a social drink and a ripe joke and juicy rumors of imminent pulpit changes, can a rabbi free himself at least momentarily from the impossibly conflicting and exalted expectations of the laymen. There are few lonelier persons than the rabbi in an isolated town a hundred miles away from his nearest colleague. With whom can he talk? Lucky is the rabbi who can relax with his *rebbetzin* (wife), provided, of course, she is not a sermon-judger. NO playwright likes to breakfast with a drama critic.

As the years since rabbinical seminary days stretch into the rabbinic menopause that refreshes, the rabbi tends to wax increasingly nostalgic about the good old student days. He even becomes sentimental about the class of '42, most of whom he couldn't abide as a student. He becomes damp-eyed about his alma mater, although as a student he organized down-with-the-seminary student revolts, coups and revolutions so militant as to make the demonstrations at Berkeley look as tame as the sisterhood fashion show.

Rabbinic Conference

There is no convention to equal a rabbinic conference. It may indeed be the most articulate assemblage in American life. It reaches the zenith of over-programing. In order to assuage the tender egos of rabbis who were not invited to present conference papers, most rabbinic conferences have now added pre-conference and post-conference sessions to allow a larger number of rabbis to

54

inflict upon each other the choicest sermon they ever
visited upon their own congregants. (The title is usually
changed from "To Do Justly" to "A Teleological Analysis
of Buberian Mysticism in the Light of the Maimonidean
Synthesis." This makes it a paper instead of a sermon.)

Competitiveness and hyperbolic escalation become
fierce, even more in the card games upstairs and in the
shoptalk in the corridors than on the floor (which is
normally drowsy). Rabbi X says to Rabbi Y: "Say, Rabbi
Z told me that he gets an average of five hundred people
to services every Shabbos. Is that possible or is he exaggerating?"

Replies Rabbi Y: "Well, I've been to Rabbi Z's services
several times. I would say he averages about three hundred people every Friday."

"Hmmm," says Rabbi X, "so he's NOT exaggerating."

The rabbi is the chief target and the main hope of
American Jewish life. And largely responsible for his becoming one or the other are synagogue lay leaders, those
usually devoted, sometimes sensitive, sometimes insuffer-
able professional volunteers who themselves live in the
fishbowl of Jewish community life. . . .

Label the Characters

(The Dramatis Personae)

MACHER	YOUNG MARRIEDS
KOCHLEFFEL	A.K. (ANCIENT KNIGHT)
NUDNIK	POTENTIAL LEADER
NEBBISH	LEADER
SHLEMIEL	

Few Jews can be pigeonholed into one of the above categories, but every chapter, club, lodge or temple has its share of them. The relative distribution of this share determines the character of the institution.

MACHER is an important layman. He is a leader by virtue of his influence, dedication and/or affluence. He is often the big giver to the building campaign and sometimes likes to announce the same single pledge publicly as often as possible. (Unlike K [see below], he even pays it.) Despite his limited knowledge of Judaism, he is tenaciously loyal to the organization and works harder for the cause than for his own business. He loves Jewish life and is hurt and distressed that his college-age son dismisses Jewish life as "vulgar and bourgeois." When his son marries out of the faith, he is humiliated and blames his wife; when the daughter-in-law converts and becomes a leading light of the sisterhood, he kvells (beams) and takes full credit. M has been to Israel ten times and cried every time. He has his shortcomings but he is a pillar of Jewish survival.

He regards the rabbi and his family as the property of the temple. When the rabbi buys a new Lincoln, M says: "We don't *need* the rabbi to be too fancy!" You can always tell who the MACHER is, because the rabbi always publicly describes him with any three of the following adjectives: indefatigable, dedicated, zealous, consecrated, beloved. How the rabbi describes him privately to the rebbetzin can only be imagined.

KOCHLEFFEL is the man or woman who stirs things up by the use of gossip, exaggeration, rumor and plot. By definition, a KOCHLEFFEL is a threat to the es-

tablishment. Say that Congregation Judea has just retained a young, unmarried rabbi. KOCHLEFFEL will
whisper to Mrs. Paramount News (the eyes and the ears
of the temple): "A nice boy, but what kind of a Jewish boy is unmarried?" Mrs. Paramount News takes it from
there. No American is more vulnerable than an unmarried
rabbi in a congregation. He must run an obstacle course
consisting of every unwed Jewish girl in town, everybody's old maid niece and every lonely Jewish widow
within a radius of three hundred miles until, in exhausted self-defense, he yields and takes a wife. When it
is rumored that the rabbi is engaged to be married, our
Mr. K asks at a men's club lox-and-bagel breakfast: "Is it
true that the rabbi is marrying an Indonesian?" The truth
is, of course, that the fiancée, Miss Ruth Ann Goldman,
recently took a trip to the Orient. "Is it true that she has
seven children by a previous marriage?" This, too, is not
true (she has seven brothers and sisters), but the tele-
phones leap throughout the community for days.

The wedding finally takes place at the temple. It is a
joyous event and the congregation is ecstatic. Except for
K: "To me she looks already pregnant." If K is powerful
as well as mischievous, he will ultimately: a) drive the
rabbi out of the *shul;* b) drive the president out of his
skull; and c) foment a split-off.

A NUDNICK may or may not be also a KOCHLEF-
FEL, but he or she is *always* a pest. N is always certain to:
a) correct the minutes; b) ask the rabbi: "You remember
me, Rabbi, what's my name?" c) refuse to pay dues to the
parent national body; d) bring Robert's Rules of Order
to the annual meeting; e) refuse to make the election

unanimous; f) hold up the Sabbath evening receiving line to tell the rabbi: "There are several points in your sermon I would like to discuss with you"; g) write monthly letters to the temple bulletin editor: "Either the Christian choir goes or I go!"; h) Say: "We must sit down and decide where we stand"; i) insist upon being recorded in the negative; j) ask: "Who authorized that?" at every opportunity; k) say: "Let's get down to the nitty-gritty." If leagued with K and A.K. (see below), N is a menace. Otherwise, he is just a pest and a living witness to the group's toleration of dissent.

A NEBBISH is a sweet nothing. He or she is certain to: a) smile uncomplainingly no matter what the disaster on all sides; b) approve everything; c) serve as chairman of the committee on time and place; d) raise his voluntary dues voluntarily on the strength of one telephone call; e) pick up all the stuff for the bazaar in his new car; f) drive the speaker to his hotel; g) read the temple bulletin from cover to cover twice; h) listen to everything K says, but fail miserably to pass it on, thus breaking the chain of communication; i) second the motion; j) belong to both temples when the split comes. In his passive way, he is an asset to the temple and acts as Neb Indian to the M Chief and sweet antidote to the K paranoia.

SHLEMIEL is a fool, not dangerous like K or pesty like N or passive like Neb, but unwittingly and unfailingly gauche. He is certain to: a) drop the prayer book in the middle of the rabbi's sermon; b) complain that he came to services but it isn't his night to usher; c) table the motion when he meant only to get the subject on the table; d) lose the speaker only six blocks from the temple;

e) drive the youth group to the game and forget where he parked the car; f) schedule the bowling tournament on the afternoon of Yom Kippur; g) blow out all the lights in the temple when changing a fuse in the middle of the drama group's presentation of *Fiddler on the Roof*; h) fall off the *succah* (the booth for the Festival of Succoth) and break his second leg (the first he broke at a rally for Soviet Jewry when he foolishly marched off by himself in the wrong direction and fell into an open manhole). SHLEMIEL should not be confused with a SHLIMAZEL. When SHLEMIEL spills hot tea, SHLIMAZEL is the one he spills it *on*. When S gets a two-pants suit, he burns a cigarette hole in his jacket. S is a nice person if he can only be kept in his place—which is home, locked in his bedroom.

YOUNG MARRIEDS are a special breed of temple members who are too old (old is your age plus ten) for the youth group and too young to die. Their principal identification with the temple is that they work hard at being youthful and married. A certain exclusiveness marks this group. They do not like unmarried people around; it makes them nervous. They do not like old people around either, especially if they are younger than the YMs themselves. Dancing, singing, discussions, weight watching, dramas and trips to Bermuda keep the YMs young and carefree. The YMs can absorb one K and one S, but more than that would set wives and husbands at each other's throats and disrupt the entire program.

A.K. (ANCIENT KNIGHT) is a person long since over the hill, but unwilling to surrender. The A.K. may well have been an M for a long time—and may be one still—

but may also develop the attributes of a K and an N in his older years. A.K. may also be in the first stages of senility, forgetting that he is only the honorary and emeritus president and not the regnant knight. Why is this knight different from all other knights? Chronological years have nothing to do with it. A.K. is often a forty-one-year-old ex-shul president. He has a tantrum anytime his name is not mentioned at an open meeting, threatening to cut the temple out of his will and to boycott the temple cemetery.

POTENTIAL LEADER is a person, preferably young, who is dynamic, articulate, knowledgeable, intellectual and well fixed. The only quality lacking in PL is some interest in our organization (a lost leader). Many organizations have tried Leadership Training, bringing PL to luncheon sessions where the techniques of group dynamics and motivation research are utilized in a dazzling succession of socio-dramas, chancel dramas, sensitivity courses, open-end discussions, verbal Rorschachs, free association and institutional half nelsons. All these modern techniques prove that the only way to make PL an M or an L is through *KOVED* (which means, roughly, feeding his ego). Koved consists of: a) naming something permanent (like the emeritus rabbi) after him; b) making him Man of the Year or, if necessary, of the Century; c) putting his picture in the newspaper; d) mentioning him in every issue of the temple bulletin; e) putting him on the board of the parent organization; f) giving him a plaque on both his houses. If you cannot make an L out of a PL, you may have a potential K or N on your hands until he is old enough to become a YM and/or an A.K. If you do succeed in making a Leader out of him, Xerox copies of him before he is stolen by the local welfare fund.

The nuclear category in Jewish life is that of the LEADER. Whether he is a paid professional or a dedicated lay volunteer, his primary task is the disbursement of koved (read patronage), the involvement of laymen (read manipulation) and the achievement of the true goals of the organization (read blood, sweat and tears). The author has spent twenty years studying this phenomenon, replete with personality, handwriting and phrenology tests, not to mention ink blots and brainwashing. The following is a composite picture based on random (believe me) sampling: The typical L is in his mid-forties, married, has two and a half children, a 1966 Buick with a dented front fender and a three-bedroom ranch house in the suburbs, near transportation. He has a flare for anonymity and does not mind (hc hates it, really, but keeps it to himself) writing eloquent speeches and reports which are ultimately delivered by some prominent lay M as his own. He attends five meetings a week, at three of which he eats corned beef on rye off a paper plate and drinks Dr. Brown's celery tonic (recently replaced by Diet-Cola) during ideological discussions of which organizations should get credit. He has been in the Jewish organizational field for ten years and during that time has written 15,673 letters and has made 876 speeches. (This does not include the time he was invited to Indianapolis to speak to a synagogue adult education group, but, since nobody else showed up, spent the evening playing gin with the rabbi.)

The typical L had, as a boy, seven or eight years of

Jewish education and he recalls that this dose of old-fashioned *cheder* (Hebrew school) was not quite potent enough to extinguish all spark of Jewish interest. He is and has always been an idealist. He had no head for business. One L took over his father's successful mortuary and worked it into the ground in six months. As a boy he dreamed of being a kibbutznik in Israel or the first Jewish President of the United States. As he got older, his aspirations rose.

How successful a Jewish organization or temple will be depends on how the pieces, described above, are deployed across the institutional chessboard. The A.K., which can move only one space at a time, should not be counted on for the attack. K moves laterally and backwards and should be surrendered early for an opposing piece. N, YM and Neb are mere pawns. S can hurt you if you're not careful. M, which moves like a queen, in all directions, has the power to lead the attack. PL must be moved forward rapidly and crowned, if at all possible. L, which moves like a horse, two steps one way and one the other, can be very helpful if he is not exposed too soon and conquered.

6. How to Build a Temple: The Jewish Edifice Complex

The American synagogue has shared fully in the religious revival which has mushroomed in the post World War II era. This revival has expressed itself most clearly in the BUILDING BOOM, known familiarly as the edifice complex. It has resulted in some of the most eye-popping edifices in Jewish history, temples which combine the worst elements of the Borgia Palace, the Astrodome and the Eiffel Tower.

Occasionally, temple building committees succumb to mass hysteria, fall under the spell of a bizarre architect who has never before been inside a synagogue (much less having designed one) and act out his and their collective fantasies. The following is the report (we hope apocryphal) of the Building Committee of Temple Gates of Blossoms, which is located in the heart of the Midwest.

Dear Mr. President:
   We want our building to be unique and to be the liberal synagogue of the future. After all,

whether we admit it or not, we ARE in competition with other congregations for membership. Let's face it: the convenience and beauty of the building is a crucial factor to potential members. The synagogue of the future should also be in harmony with the technological revolution and the automotive age. We, therefore, propose that we build a *drive-in synagogue*.

Having a drive-in synagogue will, of course, create certain problems that must be faced up to. For example, we do not want to discriminate between Cadillacs and Chevrolets, and it must be first come, first served, even for the High Holy Days. But absolute freedom will create anarchy.

Can the Widow Shmerlitz be allowed to putt-putt into the temple in that Model T Ford? Can that Yippie who is president of the Youth Group be allowed to screech in there in his hot rod? Frankly, won't people like you have to have their cars washed before coming to temple? Should a Volkswagen be *verboten?* Should we check mufflers before accepting a new member? What about multi-car families? How do we prevent necking during services? Some guidelines will have to be drawn; this *IS* a new venture. We feel, however, that that would be beyond the province of our Committee. It is a policy question. You should appoint a committee of the BIG BOARD to work out a set of guidelines on this. AND ENFORCE THEM!

Dues: Most members will continue to pay annual assessments. But what about those nonmembers who want to buy tickets only for the High Holy Days? Shall we charge by the car or by the head?

Traffic Control: A subcommittee has been puzzling over the problem of how to avoid bumper-to-bumper traffic jams in the temple, particularly at the High Holy Days, causing burst gaskets (both human and automotive). We have evolved a plan for express lanes, local lanes, semaphore signals and also for twenty-minute metered parking for those who come only for Memorial Services. If anyone honks his horn during services, there will be a master control panel on the bima and you can, by pressing a button, drop the offending car through a trap door, down an exit ramp and out onto the street before he can say "It wasn't me!"

Cost: About $700,000. It would have been more, but we're getting the marquee free from Hal Silverstone, whose drive-in movie theater burned down during a showing of *La Dolce Vita*. We are also proposing that we place open-hearth fireplaces in the shape of burning bushes at every fifth row of cars. This will counter the charge that the Reform service is cold. The question remains: how will we raise the $700,-000? Simple. We will auction the new temple to whichever caterer comes up with the highest bid. The kitchen will be modernistic, Byzantine in design, large as a football field and with sliding doors to accommodate the overflow automobiles at the High Holy Days. We figure we can have separate kitchens and hors d'oeuvre rooms, hot and cold, kosher and non-kosher, handling three Bar Mitzvahs and a wedding simultaneously. This will truly be the synagogue of the future. The caterer can advertise: "Visit Our Unique Drive-In Synagogue, Where the Posh Come to Nosh."

Rabbi: A new one to conform to the spirit of the building. This may be beyond the purview of our committee, but it must be considered by someone. Our present rabbi simply won't cut the mustard. He doesn't even drive a car. It's true, he has been with us for fourteen years, but you have to get rid of your prop plane to enter the jet age. Do we want to take off or don't we? We propose a young, swinging, dynamic rabbi. On the other hand, if we can get Rabbi Abraham Heschel, we would be pleased. He is not young, but he does have a beard, protests a lot, and would turn the kids on, especially if we can teach him to play a guitar and sing Chasidic rock-and-roll. If this should prove impossible—and we think the caterer would offer a very attractive salary to get Heschel—we have an even more daring proposal: a woman rabbi! Our survey showed that it is the women who really run the congregation anyway—and they certainly run our homes. Jewish life is matriarchal, and a male rabbi merely confuses the roles. Can we persuade our parent body and seminary to ordain women? It's worth a try. A luscious rabbi, with a quiet but nice-looking husband, would get us into *Time* Magazine and put us on the map.

The Site: Where to buy property? That is a touchy question. We have carefully studied demographic reports projecting the population patterns in which our mobile Jewish community will be moving in the decades ahead. Within ten years, almost every Jewish family will be all the way out to Highland Village, which is seventy-five miles from the city. But ten years after that, the Jewish population will start moving again. We must look ahead for many decades; after all, $700,000 is an investment of a century for all of us. Actually, how many Jews will still live in this Godforsaken part of the Midwest in the year 2000? It is so cold we have become God's frozen people! Everybody will soon be in California. We, therefore, propose that we purchase land and build our drive-in synagogue in the bay area of San Francisco. The Candlestick Drive-In Synagogue is a long way off, but so is the future.

Respectfully submitted,
THE BUILDING COMMITTEE

(by a vote of seven to two, Mr. Havelock and
Mrs. Ellis being recorded in violent
opposition, both of the view that the
rest of us have flipped . . .)

P.S. Mr. Fergessen suggested that the Candle-
stick go ecumaniacal under the name Our Lady
of the Perpetual Simcha, but there was no second, thank God.

7. How to Escape Jewish Fund-Raising
(*You Should Live So Long*)

News Item: More than six hundred Jewish leaders attended a black-tie dinner last night at the Waldorf-Astoria in New York, launching the United Jewish Appeal campaign. The minimum contribution for the event was $10,000. So many persons demanded to attend that the UJA had to move the dinner from a small ballroom at the Hilton to the Grand Ballroom at the Waldorf. Guests at the "call dinner" ate their cornish hen garni and announced their pledges of $10,000 or more for Jewish philanthropy.

This actual event, by no means extraordinary in fund-raising, confirms what all Jews—and many non-Jews—already know: American Jewry has turned fund-raising into an art. In a matter of weeks after Israel's Six-Day War in 1967, American Jews raised a half billion dollars. Jews give some $625 million to Jewish causes every year. For Jews, giving to charity is not merely philanthropic and Pavlovian; it is a religious commandment with its origins in Biblical injunctions. This old religious mandate and the ever-new Jewish heartbreak, which have tutored the hearts and purses of Jews throughout the world, make every Jew who is not made of stone an easy mark for the Jewish fund-raiser.

Jews play intricate games with fund-raising. Capturing the big givers is something like a bullfight. Everybody knows that, in the end, the bull will be conquered. But the charge lies in the beauty, the pageantry and the skill of the match. The veronica passes, the feints, the flourishes, the footwork and the timing—the elements of the chase—are what the true aficionados admire. The two or three great matadors of Jewish fund-raising inspire awed admiration; they are already living legends among Jews. One of these picks up the telephone each day to wish happy birthday to important donors throughout the country on their unlisted phones.

In Jewish fund-raising, the kill takes place at grand hotels like the Waldorf, but the true action has taken place earlier in a million private conversations in a thousand offices, health clubs, Turkish baths, country clubs, cabanas, elevators, airplanes, golf courses and synagogues. The sword is the telephone. "Max, this is Hank. As I don't have to tell you, Israel is in trouble. Yes, again. I'm doubling my pledge to the UJA. I'm counting on you to do it, too." And, "Bernie, this is Sid. Al Golden is one of your closest friends, isn't he? I thought so. We're having a dinner for him and we are counting on you to increase your pledge in his honor. I'm sure you'll want to give at least as much as Max, who hates Al's guts. It's the least we can do for Al, right?" And, "Listen, Jack, Senator Whatsisname will speak at the dinner—he's the fan dancer

—but what really counts are the pledges of the big givers to get the ball rolling. We're putting you down for ten thousand. I KNOW that's twice what you gave last year, but I bought a hundred thousand worth of goods from you this year, remember? We'll call on you first to get us off to a fast start. Thanks, pal." Every spontaneous announcement at the Waldorf has been prepared with the meticulous care which goes into the launching of a rocket. An exception was the time Moish Hernberg pledged $5000 in memory of the $25,000 he had pledged the year before.

And yet there are some ways (all unsuccessful) to try to beat the rap of Jewish fund-raising:

Dissociate Yourself

This requires a blank look and a heart of wood. Don't let yourself be swept by Jewish emotion. But don't underestimate the ultimate consequence of dissociation. It isn't easy. Merely to announce that you are not interested, do not belong to any Jewish groups or have no desire to contribute—all this is a waste of breath. To really dissociate you may have to go into hiding as a modern-day Marrano. Anywhere in America is futile. Try going abroad, but bear in mind that there are those who say the UJA has extradition treaties with most of the nations of the world.

Say You Gave at the Office

This is a very common dodge, but it rarely works. The truly effective campaigns are so well organized that they not only know whether you gave at the office but how much, when, under what duress, the effect upon your basal metabolism, how much you told your partner you gave, how much your partner told you he gave, how much you deducted from your income tax and how long your lunch hour is. Even the computer is afraid not to give to the UJA. One tried—and tilted. So don't be too cocky with this one. It's a boomerang.

Stand on Principle

Denounce the entire campaign as contrary to the principles of equal justice. If your organization ran a deficit last year (and it did), say: "If God wanted man to live on a deficit budget, he would have made ink red instead of black. After all, why should a few of us (be sure to say US, not YOU) have to carry the heaviest burden of the campaign year after year, while several of the members WHO CAN AFFORD TO GIVE MUCH MORE THAN WE CAN get by with peanuts? The only way to remedy this injustice is to put the facts on the line! *I'm* not embarrassed to publish my gift and I would certainly like to know why anybody else should be embarrassed!" Wind up with a blister: "Gentlemen, what are we trying to do here—give to save Jews or protect some fat cats among us from giving what they *should?*"

Then storm out of the room saying: "I HAVE HAD IT! ON ME YOU SHOULD NOT RELY!" (This performance may win you an Oscar, maybe even a reprieve of a few weeks while the controversy smokes, and you may pick up an extra plaque to sweeten your ultimate surrender. But you don't have a chance.) Moreover, it is not always possible to storm out. Sometimes they tie your shoelaces together and bolt the door.

Wax Philosophical

This is a sophisticated gambit. Speak in a wise, weary voice, something like this: "Gentlemen, I'm as good a Jew as any of you, I think you'll have to admit. As you all know, I give ten thousand dollars anonymously every year. But times have changed. The day of sectarian giving is over. This is an ecumenical, transdenominational era. Take Brandeis University. What's Jewish about it? The student body is non-sectarian, as it should be. The curriculum is secular, as it should be. So what's Jewish? The money? Why? Or take the Jewish Hospital. What's Jewish about it? It's open to everyone, regardless of race and religion. So what if it has a kosher kitchen? So does St. Joseph's Catholic Hospital. We've got to get rid of this sectarian system and the place to start is fund-raising. Why must I give as a Jew? Why not as a human being, an American, a compassionate man of the world? You see, gentlemen, I admire what you have done for so many years. But let us face it, in the days of the welfare state you are now as anachronistic as animal sacrifices in the temple."

A potent and intriguing argument will prevail until Dave, the chairman, fixes you with: "Okay, okay, Sam, very pretty. You're as full of it as a Thanksgiving goose. So I'm putting you down for the same as last year." Dave may also give you twenty lashes with a wet pledge card.

Become the Chairman

As chairman, you can try this ingenious escape route: "Being chairman of this campaign takes a tremendous number of man-hours. Figure out what my time is worth. That's my contribution—it's worth a fortune." It is a noble delusion. By the time the journal is in preparation, the pledges are being readied and the screws are applied, you will not only give your time but you will find yourself decked out in a shiny tuxedo at the big dinner, standing at the microphone in front of a four-tier dais and announcing to an admiring throng: "As chairman, and in tribute to the wonderful support you have all given me this year, I am proud to announce that I am doubling my pledge." Pandemonium. Applause. The old Bar Mitzvah glow all over again. And another unsuccessful "out" fades into oblivion.

Biblical Text

There is one other way—not to escape Jewish fundraising exactly, but to get your money's worth. The story is told of Mr. and Mrs. Jake Finegelt, who, enjoying their summer vacation, visited the nearby temple. A fundraising meeting was going on to secure funds for a new building. Each person filled out a pledge card and passed it up to the chairman, who then announced it. A deeply loyal Jew, Finegelt decided to add his contribution. He made the pledge card out for $100 and passed it forward. "Isn't this nice," announced the chairman, beaming, "here's a wonderful couple, not even members, who are contributing to our building fund. MR. AND MRS.

FINEGELT PLEDGE FIVE HUNDRED DOLLARS!"

The Finegelts were upset, but they were too embarrassed to say anything, because the congregation burst into applause. Afterward, Mr. Finegelt rushed up to the chairman to protest that he had only pledged $100, not $500. The chairman apologized for the error but he said Finegelt should have corrected him earlier. How would it look to announce the change now? Mr. Finegelt was not assuaged.

"Tell you what," said the chairman. "You keep it at $500, and to make it up to you, we'll put your favorite passage from the Bible over the entrance to the new building. Wouldn't that be an honor? That way, your gift will live forever. You just let me know which passage."

Finegelt reluctantly agreed. He and his wife went home to look through the hotel Bible. Next day they returned and supplied the text (now handsomely inscribed over the portal of a New England synagogue): "I came to you a stranger, and you took me in."

What would happen if government got wise enough to utilize the techniques of Jewish fund-raising? What if, for example, New York City tried to wipe out its oppressive deficits by drawing on the experience tested in the United Jewish Appeal? Let's see . . .

8. How to Give to New York City—Or We'll Close It!*

Given that sure-fire slogan, all that's needed are the practiced techniques of Jewish fund-raising such as the following:

Kol Nidre Appeal

Every synagogue in the New York metropolitan area should have a New York City Appeal along with the United Jewish Appeal, Bond and Federation drives. The mayor, or one of his representatives, should be invited on Kol Nidre to make an appeal in behalf of New York City. This appeal should explain why we need New York City, what it does for Jewish life, how many jobs it makes available and how it has more Jews than all of Israel, so it must be doing something right.

Name it After Me

Every synagogue should have a Big Gifts lox-and-bagel breakfast (preferably in a country club, not at the

* This article appeared originally in *Congress Weekly* and is reprinted with permission.

shul) in behalf of New York City. For gifts of $100,000 or more, the name of the donor should be memorialized in various departments and agencies of New York City. Examples; the Rebecca Goldfarb Independent Subway; the Shlomo Kertz Public Library; the Stern Family Department of Correction.

New York is Good for the Jews

Since it is important to reach the rank and file and not just the big giver, the membership of the temple should be divided up by the New York City Appeal Committee and each member should be visited at his home or place of business so that the great needs of New York City can be brought home (or to his office) to him. The block captain himself must be well versed in making the sales pitch in behalf of the city. For example, the following opening is strongly recommended: "Listen, Abe (the informal approach), I know you are familiar with New York City. You are a very generous chap and have never turned away a needy cause. I am here to talk to you about our New York City Appeal. We may have to close the city. We need money desperately. We are short of water. Our air, streets, subways and plays are dirty. Our schools, when we have them open, are overcrowded. We are losing our newspapers one by one; the New York *Post* is the only good English-Jewish newspaper left. The Long Island Expressway is the biggest parking lot in the world. In sports we have more teams and enjoy them less. Central Park you can't walk around except inside a Sherman tank. So we are running an emergency campaign. It will take five hundred million dollars. Figure the best you can do, then double it. What do you mean, is it good for the Jews? Tell me, when you hear somebody from the South or the Midwest attacking New York City, don't you know in your heart he's an anti-Semite? So how can we let the city down?"

Field the Curves

The block captains must be briefed so that they can field the curves with which the potential donor always tries to fend off the fund-raiser. For example, he will throw things like this: Why should I give to New York City? What did it ever do for me? . . . Doesn't New York City duplicate the work of other big cities? . . . I gave at the office. . . . My wife gave in Scarsdale. . . . If I give to New York City, first thing you know Los Angeles and Miami Beach will be after me. . . . Thirty years ago, a cop gave me a traffic ticket; I wouldn't give a cent to New York City. . . . I'm really over-subscribed this year. . . . Philosophically I'm opposed to New York City. . . . I'd be glad to contribute, but I'm giving to the United States Appeal.

Mobilize the Women

In the spirit of ecumenism, the synagogues and churches and universities should join together and organize a Friends of New York City. The slogan could be: "You don't have to be a Quaker to be a Friend of New York City." The first thing this organization should do is to organize women's chapters. That's where the money is. The Friends of New York should distribute black and blue *pushkes* to women and children who will stand in front of the theaters at night and yell: "Give to New York City!" Interreligious teams—be sure to include a black Greek Orthodox plus a Protestant, Catholic and Jew—should buttonhole Long Island commuters at Penn Station and Westchester commuters at Grand Central and should sing catchy ditties like:

> Do you think it is fair
> To consume our water and air,
> To take but not to give,
> To live but not let live,
> Then to take your riches
> Back to Center Moriches?
> Have a little pity
> On New York City.

Over the Top

New York City could become a very good campaign, not as good as a big disease or as magnetic as Israel, but better than, say, the Jewish Committee for the Birch Society. Full-page ads in the New York *Times* showing life in New York City as it really is could tear at the heartstrings like the HIAS refugee ads. A telethon, with Richard Tucker saying Kaddish for New York City, is good for an over-the-top drive. Remember that card-calling is embarrassing, unethical and very effective. So try it.

Reward the Giver

Nobody gives something for nothing. Each giver should be given at least a token gift. In fact, for $5.00 or less, one should be given a subway token. For $50, a tank of clean air. For $1000, a judgeship. Anybody who is responsible for raising over $100,000 for New York City should be given a truly exciting gift, comparable to UJA's free trip to Israel. Perhaps a home in Larchmont!

9. How to Translate Jewish Public Relations

Every Jewish organization must have a P.R. man. It is as indispensable as a deficit budget and a mimeograph machine. The first Jewish P.R. man in recorded history stood at Moses' side before he ascended Mt. Sinai. The P.R. man said: "Look, Moses, if you can pull this off, I can get you four pages in the Bible." To be a modern Jewish P.R. man, you must have a variety of talents. You must know how to write a press release, frame a speech, communicate with several publics, invent a gimmick, worry out loud, play it by ear, draft articles that appear in the name of your chairman, cry a lot, tear a passion, fashion a fund-raising program, curse in Yiddish, stay ahead of the competition, holler, know all about feedback and flak, make up good excuses when skunked by the New York *Times* and dream up TV and radio programs (which will appear Sundays at 6 A.M.) to put your organization in the limelight. These are SOP, but the most important talents required of you, if you wish to make it as a Jewish P.R. man, are the following:

Manage the Membership Figures

Just as the CIA doesn't give away its secret codes, no Jewish organization gives away its true membership totals. Keep it flexible. If it's 300,000, describe it as "nearing 500,000." If your opposition organization claims "approximately a million members," claim a membership "exceeding 1,100,000." Nobody knows the true body count anyway, including you, because your local groups won't tell you, so remember that membership is a function of public relations. Membership never declines. How fast it advances depends on your competition . . . and your imagination.

Cultivate the Fellow on the "Jewish Beat"

Everybody knows that newspapers are objective, print all the news that fits and judge every story on its merits. Of course, but if Matty Gross likes you, your stories will prove more meritorious than the competition's. From time to time, send Matty Rosh Hashanah and Lag b'Omer cards, a volume of Keats poems, an occasional statuette of Isaiah, and hot tips on the races and stocks. When you are with Matty, laugh hysterically at his Yiddish jokes (never let him find out you don't understand Yiddish), and don't interrupt his monologues. If sometimes he's too busy to see you, don't pout. Remember, he's got thirty-six other Jewish P.R. men "cultivating him" too—it's a wonder you haven't all plowed him under already!

Involve Your Laymen

This is very important. It is vital to have a committee of the top laymen in your movement who are experts in advertising and public relations. It is even more vital not to convene any meetings of this committee, because they will want you to prepare cockamamy multicolored diagrams, charts and audio-visual presentations about all the strata of your various publics. They will also want to devise ways to "involve" laymen in every phase of your organization's work. Don't do it. The only thing worse than an uninvolved laity is an involved laity. You'll never get any work done. There is really only one way to involve laymen and it is called koved. Give each layman a statuette of Isaiah, a plaque or a scroll, preferably laminated. Don't forget to allocate koved to the members of the P.R. committee, too, because they're furious that you never call a meeting. They never know that the road to inertia is paved with committee meetings.

Don't Confuse P.R. with Reality

Your best news breaks have nothing to to with what happens on the floor of the conventions. They are dreamed up by you and Matty in the hotel press room in the warm afterglow of a steak dinner and two bottles of chablis. The delegates on the floor are dully debating a hike in dues, but you and Matty, hunched over a smoking typewriter, are brainstorming a hot story on the Bar Mitzvah of Jesus or challenging Nasser to a duel in the sun. When you hit a ripe story, you can milk it at least once a year. One organization announced a new art program seven times. When they actually started the program ten years later, the papers wouldn't print it and the P.R. man was fired.

Once you have worked up the "language," the question

is whose mouth to put it into. Be careful. The chairman of your P.R. committee is out to cut you off at the knees, so put the "language" in his mouth. But if the papers play him big, you'd better have a good explanation for your executive director. He's not a publicity hound exactly, but he's still waiting for you to get him on the cover of *Time*.

Don't Unpack

Your profession has a very rapid turnover. If you have an assistant, your tenure is even more precarious. If your organization has a sabbatical plan and you have an assistant, don't take the sabbatical. Insofar as promotions are concerned, there is not much room to move vertically. The direction of growth is circular (spin your wheels until you get tenure) and horizontal—over to a bigger organization which will pay you $2000 more per year, partly as recompense for the secrets you bring over from the competition, partly for your relationship with Matty. The best way to know your status in your organization is to ask yourself the following questions:

A. Do you have a carpet in your office?
B. A private phone?
C. Are you invited to top staff meetings?
D. Do they pass notes to you during these meetings?
E. Do you have a key to the men's room?
F. Is your name on the letterhead?
G. Do you see the top man at least once a week (not counting the men's room)?
H. What floor is your office on? How many windows?

I. How many credit cards do you have?

J. How many Isaiah statuettes did they give you?

K. What does the receptionist call you behind your back?

Be Jaded

You have to develop a weary, jaundiced demeanor, even if you're only twenty-five years old. This is no field for bright eyes and oh gees. The look of ennui will conceal the fact that deep down you're shallow. Be cool. Your characteristic response to new ideas should be: "Oy, you want to trot out *that* dog again?" Or: "That's good for a giggle." Or: "That's got all the pizzazz of a warmed-over potato knish." Or: "It's a bomb, but Matty owes me one. Maybe we can fog a paragraph past the city desk. It'll be my mazel [luck] they'll use the damn thing."

The Saga Of T. L. Shmeikel

One of the most successful and colorful characters of the Jewish P.R. fraternity was T. L. Shmeikel. He wore a red vest to work every day, summer and winter, and spats on rainy days. He smoked nothing but Havana cigars, like the Pierre Salinger of the Jewish bureaucracy. T.L. was a living legend in the field. He drove a red Volkswagen, presided over lunch at Voisin and ran through four wives and seven secretaries in ten years. He always operated on all cylinders and, since his mind raced faster than his words, his words came tumbling out like double-talk. Phumphking, it was called in the trade. He typed with two fingers at a phenomenal clip. Everybody knew that T.L. could write up a storm, but he couldn't spell. His secretary, therefore, had to have three talents: 1) a mastery of spelling; 2) an ability to interpret his phumphking; and 3) big breasts.

T.L. was paranoid. He always thought people were out to fire him. As long as anyone could remember, T.L. was under analysis. His analyst persuaded him that people *were* out to fire him and "besides, anybody who is not paranoid these days is crazy." T.L. would run out in the middle of a press conference phumphking, "Geez, I'm late for the goddam shrink!" He saw his head shrinker three times a week. After ten years of analysis, nobody could detect a scintilla of change in T.L., but it was said that his analyst, who had now become an authority on Jewish P.R., was beginning to phumphke. Then T.L. discovered the new field of sensitivity training, broke with his shrink in a terrible scene at the Y gym and became a chasid for group sensitivity training.

T.L.'s most brilliant idea was, as the New York *Times* religion page put it, to "create a revolutionary synthesis between the dynamics of ancient Judaism and the insights of modern sensitivity programming." He came up with the notion of taking fourteen of his organization's board members away for a pilot weekend of candid self-searching and mutual understanding. The press loved it. *Look* did a two-page picture feature on it. *Time* called it a "new breakthrough in religion." *Reader's Digest* published T.L.'s piece entitled "The Most Unforgettable Weekend of My Life." Huntley and Brinkley did seven minutes on "Religion and Inner Space—the Story of a Weekend." The publicity was sensational. What actually transpired at the weekend, on the other hand, was a pogrom. The group spent twenty of the thirty-six hours eating. Then they argued for three hours as to whether to impose a five-minute rule on each speaker. In the remaining time, instead of baring their individual souls and sitting in the mud in the nude, they drew up impeachment papers against the organization's president. After the weekend, when the president heard about the proceedings, T.L. was cashiered, thus demonstrating that he was not really paranoid after all.

T.L. is now a professional sensitivity training leader. And his shrink is now the P.R. director of the organization. The moral of the story is, as Matty Gross put it, "If you want to go places in P.R. like T.L., shrink big!"

The Press Room

While Matty is very important to you (no more than, say, oxygen), you must not let him push you around. You must handle yourself with authority. You are not, after all, a mere press agent; you are a public relations director. Try to remember that. The following conversation, which is alleged to have taken place between Matty and a brand-new P.R. director of a large organization in the press room at a convention hotel, is undoubtedly apocryphal. It demonstrates the proper give-and-take relationship of mutual respect between the press and the P.R. officer:

Matty (bursting into the press room): "Okay, kiddo, I just talked to my editor. He wants eight paragraphs, but hard news, no *shtuss*, you hear? Okay now, so what's the scenario? How many delegates you got here?"

"We've registered exactly three hundred and seventeen delegates," the P.R. man said.

Matty (shouting): "I can't announce three hundred seventeen delegates, kiddo! My editor will laugh at me. Okay, it's seven hundred! Order me a sandwich. I can't work on an empty stomach. Now, how many days will this dreary seance here go on?"

"It's a one-day conference."

Matty (furious): "A ONE-DAY CONFERENCE! My editor would think I'm crazy, coming three thousand miles for a one-day meeting. I'm starved. What's keeping that anti-Semitic room service? Okay, so it's a three-day convention. We'll need two more A.M. stories."

"I sent you an advance release. Maybe we can—"

Matty plops down on a chair and begins pounding away at a battered typewriter. "Your release stinks. Where did you learn your journalism—the White Anglo Saxon Hebrew (WASH) Home for Unwed Mothers? There. *That's* the lead. Now, what are the delegates talking about now?"

"I'm not sure. Should we go out on the floor and find out?"

Matty (red-faced and drawing himself up to his full and furious 6′2″): "Listen, kiddo. I've been covering these Jewish happenings for twenty-five years and I never—do you hear me, NEVER—go out on the floor! Now, when is that cockamamy debate about federal aid to education going to unfold?"

P.R. man consults the printed program. "Here it is. It goes on at eight tonight."

Matty (leaping onto the table and waving his long arms hysterically): "ARE YOU OUT OF YOUR KOP, BABY? I'VE GOT AN EARLY DEADLINE! YOU HEAR ME? THAT DEBATE GOES ON THIS AFTERNOON AT TWO! ARE YOU TRYING TO KILL ME?"

And, of course, the debate went on at 2 P.M. It was very exciting. Matty, needless to say, was not there. He was in the press room, happily feeding on the new P.R. man.

When the history of American Jewish life is finally written, the deathless prose of Matty and his fellows will provide the raw material. And the history will be written, of course, on mimeograph paper.

Vocabulary

To master the vocabulary of Jewish public relations, you have to be able to separate the press release from what really happened, as for instance:

The Release	*The Reality*
A membership of approximately 50,000 members . . .	20,000.
Some 200 delegates gathered at the Fontainebleau today for the opening. . . .	75—everybody else at the dog races.
A spot check of the delegates revealed today . . .	Matty talked to the P.R. man, his secretary and a man in the men's room.

92

Mr. Asa Shmendrick, chairman of the board, urged the organization to concentrate its energies and resources on the strengthening and deepening of Jewish identity and Jewish education.

Shmendrick wants us to lay off civil rights.

The spokesman, in a reference to the urban crisis, said: "Both American and Jewish history demonstrate that the only true way for a minority to achieve dignity and strength is not violence or breast-beating, but education, hard work and self-help."

Why can't Negroes be more like Jews?

The two Jewish philanthropic agencies announced that a full merger agreement had been worked out. "Seven years of joint study had finally overcome the ideological and philosophic barriers which had inhibited the joining of forces."

Jacques Ferbissener, the president, died.

The Fund announced a $15-million emergency campaign.

Five million bigger than last year's emergency.

Temple Vasich Vus announced today that 50 per cent of its building fund goal of $500,000 was already subscribed.

The committee sold half the temple to the caterer.

The Youth Committee today unveiled a six-point program to "better involve Jewish youth in the life of the congregation."

We put color television in the youth lounge.

The leader of several international Jewish organizations, Dr. Nachmanides Silvermensh is known as an articulate spokesman for virtually every Jewish cause.

When will Silvermensh learn the difference between greetings and remarks?

In a press conference today, the Jewish Foundation announced it was joining forces with the Catholic Church in an Ecumenical Center on Christian-Jewish Relations.

If you can't beat 'em, join 'em.

10. How to Visit Israel—and Get Back Home

The State of Israel represents something profound, emotional and deeply mysterious for Jews throughout the world. It represents a Jewish do-it-yourself triumph over the assaults of history, refuting the mockeries of the centuries. Perhaps it will not always be so for Jews (the younger generation is losing this sense already), but for Jews who remember the day when the blue and white Israeli flag first fluttered over Tel Aviv in 1948, Israel will never cease to be a source of pride, awe and astonishment.

Israel is perhaps the most visceral aspect of modern Jewish identification. It is the undoubted magnet of Jewish fund-raising. Israel, with its dramatic human problems, draws the bulk of Jewish contributions throughout the world, although the funds are divided among a host of overseas and domestic needs. If there were no Israel, Jewish fund-raising would have to create one. Indeed, in one sense it may be argued that that is almost what happened.

Visiting Israel is not only an adventure, it is also a primary form of Jewish identification—even of status. The first act of the ritual is landing on El Al at Lod (Lydda) Airfield near Tel Aviv. Upon his first trip, the Jewish visitor is flooded with emotion and often weeps with unashamed ecstasy. He feels better when they finally recover his bags. Marveling at things Jewish is the mark of the first visit. (Just think! A Jewish airplane! Look! a Jewish customs man! Imagine! A Jewish hotel! Taste . . . a Jewish ice cream! Drink . . . a Jewish soda pop! Shave . . . a Jewish shaving cream! Listen . . . a Hebrew *La Traviata!* Would you believe . . . a Jewish cop! Buy it . . . an Israeli dress! Eat . . . a Jewish corn-on-the-cob! Oy . . . a Jewish dysentery!!)

Eat, Eat

Eating is one of the games Jews play in Israel (and everywhere else, for that matter). Simple but lavish is the rule. The most unusual meal is breakfast. It consists of herring, tuna fish, cucumbers, tomatoes, black and green olives, fruit, sour cream, eggs, goat's cheese and bad coffee, and it lasts until lunch. Other meals are plentiful and, while they are nothing to write home about, everything that happens to the tourist in Israel proves to be something to write home about. The highest achievement in eating is to eat something uniquely Israeli, like *daggim min hayam* (fish from the sea). Dining in a small fish restaurant in Jaffa, overlooking the Mediterranean, may not be as tasty as Captain Starn's in Atlantic City, but did King Solomon's ships ever dock in Atlantic City?

The Telephone

Another wondrous game for the tourist in Israel is using the telephone. Indeed, the telephone should be approached as a game, like Monopoly, or a contest, like the public lottery, and certainly not as a form of communication. For the telephone system in Israel, owing either to a shortage of equipment or the perversity of Israeli telephone operators, or both, can prove either to be a source of hilarity, if one has the temperament for it, or a provocation to jump off the roof of the King David Hotel. The telephone, like everything in Israel except the Army, doesn't work very well.

The following is a (barely) fictional account of one recent telephone attempt by an American tourist in a Haifa hotel.

"Hello, operator?"

"You expected somebody else?"

"Well, no. I would like to call Mr. Benno Fine, here in Haifa. I don't have the address. Would you look it up for me?"

"He doesn't live in Haifa."

"Operator, please look it up. You didn't look it up."

"Okay, okay, I will call you back."

Fifteen minutes elapse. The operator calls back.

"Benjamin Cohen moved to Jerusalem. He couldn't stand the sea."

"What Benjamin Cohen? I said Benno Fine. B-E-N-N-O F-I-N-E."

"Why didn't you say so? I will look." Clicks off.

Twenty minutes elapse.

"I have for you Bingo Quinn."

"What Bingo Quinn? BENNO FINE! BENNO FINE!"

(Muttering softly) "Oy, another American *meshugener* [crazy one]. I'll get back at you." Clicks off.

"Tell me something. Mr. Klein has a sister in Haifa?"

"I don't know. It's Fine. F-I-N-E. BENNO."

"You said Benno. That's a Jewish name? Benno? I should live so long. Wait. I will ring him."

An hour passes.

"You asked for Benno Fine? He lives now in Tel Aviv."

"Good, operator. Will you ring him for me now?"

"He has no telephone. Could I give you instead a Moshe Fink?"

Trees

Another game which American tourists play in Israel is visiting their trees. Israel is being carved out of the ruins of ancient desert and rock. One of the first necessities of development was to irrigate the parched land and to cultivate the areas which had lain waste for centuries. One solution: trees. The Jewish National Fund (JNF) planted groves in millions of dunams of Israel. This was accomplished by persuading Jews throughout the world to buy trees in Israel. Hardly a Jewish child in America does not own a tree in one of the rising forests of the Holy Land. His mother carried the blue and white JNF box before she carried him. Trees have helped to make the desert bloom like a rose.

No sooner does a visiting Jew land in Israel but he wants to see his own tree. Standing over his tiny seedling in the Lower Galilee he feels himself rooted to the new land.

If you are a macher, particularly if you have made a large contribution to JNF, the visit to your trees is not optional. You will be ambushed in the lobby of the King David Hotel (there are those who believe that the reception committee is the same group which kidnapped Eichmann in Argentina, but this is a canard), piled into a jeep and driven straight up the side of a mountain at a speed certain to bring the blood to your head and your heart to your throat. If you have a fear of heights, forget it, because the driver is a fierce young Zionist who grew up in Milwaukee and became an Israeli and, out of principle, will not converse in English. If the jeep (and you) survive the ascent, you will be yanked out of the car, stood up in front of a sign that was quickly painted over with your name while you were making your *aliyah* up the mountain, photographed next to the sign and in front of ten unpromising seedlings (the photographer has you stand on your knees so that the trees will tower over you), whisked back into the jeep, dropped like an anchor down the mountainside and returned to your still-warm seat on the couch at the King David. Within a week, the picture will appear in your hometown newspaper, your temple bulletin, your Anglo-Jewish weekly and in the mailbox of your older brother, who has not yet bought a grove in Israel.

See That?

See That? is a wonderful game which can only be played by persons who have been in Israel before, preferably (but not necessarily) a few years ago. To play See That?, one points out the window to a lush orange grove as the car bumps toward Mitula and proclaims: "SEE THAT? When I was first in Israel that was nothing but a malarial swamp. Look at it now! What an amazing country." Or one slams on the brakes overlooking the bustling port town of Ashdod: "SEE THAT? When I was here just three years ago, that was nothing but sand as far as the eye could see. Today? The second largest port in Israel. Tomorrow? Biggest port in the Middle East! Amazing country!" "SEE THAT? When I was last in Beersheba, I visited the camel market. Now it's gone and they only have a camel for tourists behind the Desert Inn Hotel." "SEE THAT? That's the Bedouin going to the Desert Inn on his motor scooter to take care of his camel!" "SEE THAT? When I was here last that was Syria. Now it's Ramat Golan!" Or you are visiting a dusty kibbutz in the Negev. "SEE THAT white-thatched old man walking in the pasture? When I was here last, he was the Prime Minister! An amazing country!" "SEE THAT new building at Hebrew University? When I was here last it was just being planned as a tribute to the great American writer, Lester Malkowitz from Denver." Malkowitz? What did he write? "A check! What an amazing country!"

Dig We Must

The most "in" activity in Israel is joining a "dig." Much of the country threatens to be disemboweled in the search for artifacts from biblical days. The prestigious tourist may be invited to join one of the famous digs at

Masada, Megiddo or Capernaum. (If you're smart, grab a dig working on the seventh century, c.e.; all the other centuries are already used up.) One may not be fortunate enough to find a new Dead Sea Scroll or the nightgown of Bathsheba or Esau's razor, but one will certainly be awed by the mystical confluence of antiquity and modern life. One will stand on soil where civilization was born, where ancient armies clashed, where prophets cried out and where man first stirred to God's commandments.

But the most resourceful archeological adventure is do-it-yourself. This is not easy, because the government frowns on it. Yet, with imagination and a spade, one can have his own expedition. We know a man who spent six months digging up a wadi in the outskirts of Jerusalem. At the bottom of the wadi, he uncovered an underground cell of Reform Jews, the modern-day Marranos of Israel, praying quietly away from the unsuspecting eye of the Orthodox Establishment (who regard non-Orthodox Jews as falling somewhere between lepers and Cossacks). Unsure of himself, he threw them back.

Religious Freedom

In 1968, Reform Jews planned a "pray-in" at the Western Wall (Wailing Wall) in Jerusalem. In response, the ultra-Orthodox organized vigilantes to stone the "invaders," who planned to have men and women pray together. Israeli government officials, fearless in the face of Arab aggression, chewed their nails. Say, the government leaders suggested to Reform leaders, it's no good you Reform Jews getting stoned at the Wall. It would be used by the Arabs against Israel.

So the Reformers put off their pray-in, the ultras put down their rocks, the Israeli officials relaxed and went back to the easier business of coping with the Arabs and the Jewish state continued, in characteristic Jewish style, to extend full religious liberty in Israel to everyone . . . except Jews.

Aliyah

A major problem in Israel is that of ALIYAH (going to Israel to live). In pre-Israeli days, Zionism was a dynamic, world-wide movement whose goal was the creation of a Jewish national homeland in Palestine. In 1948, to the surprise of many leading Zionists and others, the goal was achieved. From then on, nobody could ever figure out what a Zionist was. Some say a Zionist is a Jew who tries to persuade a second Jew to give money to settle a third Jew in Israel. Zionism has become an ideal whose time has gone. Is a Zionist now someone who is friendly to Israel? Well, so are the non-Zionists—indeed, all Jews, not to mention WASP candidates for public office in America. Is a Zionist someone who contributes to Israel? Well, as Ben Gurion puckishly used to remind the Zionists, the non-Zionists give even more. So what is a Zionist? The Israelis (understandably worried that Israel is becoming an oriental or Levantine state) have a simple answer: if you claim to be a Zionist, you must come and live in Israel. The result is a thunderous silence. Aw, come on, say the Israelis, stop playing games, we need you. The silence now becomes eloquently ominous. But the number of Americans who come to stay continues to be a small trickle (and many of *them* finally trickle back) and an even larger number of Israelis come to the United States for extended visits (for many, these visits have already lasted as long as the State of Israel).

So aliyah has not worked out. Every year there is an eyeball-to-eyeball dialogue between Israeli leaders and American Jewish leaders in Jerusalem. The dialogue goes roughly like this:

Israeli: Why don't you come to live in Israel?

American: Oy, here we go again!

I: We need your Western skills and education, you know. We need more Jews here! If you don't come, we may have to ban the birth control pill here!

A: We like it in America.

I: What like? Here you can be full Jews!

A: What full Jews? Here I would be discriminated against if I were non-Orthodox. In America I am free to choose.

I: What choose? So you will choose to assimilate. Big deal!

A: What assimilate? We will still be Jews long after you have lost all Jewish religious spirit here. You will be Israelis, not Jews.

I: What Jews? You have the KKK and black anti-semites. Some day you will have pogroms and then it will be too late.

A: What pogroms? If pogroms ever come to America, Israel will not be safe either.

I: What safe? All you Americans want is peace, happiness and comfort!

A: And what do you want?

I: What should we want? Peace, happiness and comfort.

The dialogue is always concluded in a spirit of near-riot, with mutual congratulations for the "candor of our exchange, speaking heart to heart as brother Jews." The theme for the next dialogue: ALIYAH. The annual dialogue allows the American Jews to plan another visit to Israel, because—let's face it—to American Jews Israel is a nice place to visit and one of the most delightful games Jews play.

Play Visiting Israel Properly (VIP)

1. I have been to Israel

    a) not yet.
    b) ten times.
    c) as well as Italy and Ireland (I'm a politician).
    d) for the FBI.

2. Sabra is

    a) a female saber.
    b) Hebrew for "you don't look Jewish."
    c) a native-born Israeli.
    d) a death-defying driver of a Tel Aviv auto-boos.

3. Aliyah is

    a) a nose bob.
    b) driving straight up a mountain to see your tree.
    c) no problem is too small to baffle us.

d) a new town created this morning in the Negev.

e) aw, come on.

4. Tel Aviv is

a) a modern sand dune.

b) tell me, what has Portnoy got to complain?

c) nickname for a Jewish virgin from Beersheba.

d) Israel's largest city.

5. A *sheroot* is

a) an American Zionist trying to get back to America.

b) an African medicine man studying animal husbandry in Safed.

c) a cigar.

d) a collective taxicab.

6. Davidka is the

a) lineal descendant of King David.

b) an Israeli cannon.

c) Dayan's name for Ben Gurion.

d) inventor of Kosher chicken chow mein.

7. A kibbutz is

a) heckling the card game.

b) a graduate student at Hebrew University.

c) a tree visited by Marjorie Morningstar and her two French poodles.

d) Hebrew for "eat, my child."

e) a collective farm where Jews work all day, argue all night, and produce the largest crop of memos per capita of any farmers in the world.

8. El Al is

a) a flying delicatessen.

b) an Egyptian eunuch.

c) an idiot surveyor who drew the armistice borders.

d) the favorite son of Mama Loshen.

e) the only airline in the world where passengers walk the aisles all the way across the ocean.

9. The Jerusalem *Post* is

a) a post office.

b) a hitching station for full-blooded Israeli horses.

c) a newspaper.

d) Journalist record of short wars and long speeches.

Give yourself nine points for every correct answer. We know that 11×9=99. Look, nobody's perfect.

Climbing the Status Ladder to Israel

1. I have been to Israel.
2. I saw the Chagall windows.
3. I was *not* there as part of an organized group.
4. I have been more than three times.
5. I stayed in a pension.
6. I was provided with a limousine and a guide (not at my expense).
7. I was introduced to the President and/or the Prime Minister.
8. I was mentioned in the Jerusalem *Post*.
9. I lived on a kibbutz for more than a month.
10. I was there long enough to learn to speak Hebrew.
11. I felt guilty that I didn't stay there permanently.
12. I came back and made speeches about Israel.
13. I came back and wrote articles about Israel.
14. I came back and wrote a book about Israel.
15. I came back and criticized Israel.

If you climb as high as two, you're still an amateur tourist. If you got to three, you're on your way. Four means you have a future, keep shimmying. Five means you're reckless. Six means the Jewish Agency confused you with a big giver. Seven means you're a name-dropper. Eight means you've arrived as a social climber. Nine means you are for real. Ten is an achievement. Eleven, it's about time. Twelve, of course. Thirteen, why not? Fourteen, we'd be more impressed if it were in Hebrew. Fifteen, you've hit the summit. *L'hitraot* (until we meet again).

11. How to Be a Jewish Liberal
(*Despite Everything*)

Jews are one of the most liberal segments of white America. Public opinion polls demonstrate that Jews are more favorably disposed to civil rights, civil liberties, the United Nations and the welfare state than perhaps any other religious or ethnic group. The Wassermann test of Jewish liberalism in the United States is civil rights. Even after they made it in America and became Exhibit A of successful minority group adjustment, Jews continued to be obsessed by the plight of the Negro. The Negro became the conscience of the Jew. The two were—and are—tied together in a tangled skein of ambivalences, mutual dependencies, common aspirations, resentments and alliances.

Jews are still racial liberals and the polls confirm the liberal Jewish vote, the high level of Jewish contributions to and memberships in civil rights organizations. (Of course, this was truer before the New York school hassle, but it still exists.) But there is a rub. Jews, by and large, don't live with Negroes. Jews, for the most part, don't really know Negroes on a peer-to-peer, human basis. And their children go to schools that are, largely, white and homogenized. The result is that Jewish racial and economic liberalism has a peculiar hang-up: Jews don't have Negroes or poor people to be liberal with. It's a challenge.

But since racial liberalism is almost the touchstone of "the good Jew" in modern America, there are ways to circumvent this terrible dilemma. The following is a contemporary scale for Jewish liberalism on the racial front:

Compensatory Program

You get one point for your personal "compensatory treatment" program. It goes like this: You are whipping your car down the parkway—as always, under a full head of steam and late for the office. A small car suddenly darts over and cuts you off and then the driver slows to a creep in front of you. You boil over. The moment you can, you pull your car alongside of his, angrily roll down your window, a furious insult forming on your lips and about to be launched until . . . oy, he's a Negro! You stare at him, blankly, the poised obscenity freezing on your lips. He stares at you wonderingly. Finally, he yells: "WHAT'SA MATTER, MAN, HAVEN'T YOU EVER SEEN A VOLVO BEFORE?"

Integrate Your Home

You get two points for feeling guilty that you live in a segregated neighborhood, three points for telling your neighbor that you would be pleased if he sold his home to a Negro, four if you sell your *own* home to a non-white (but minus three if it is only because you had a foolish fight with the shlemiel next-door whose dog for ten long years had done his business on your lawn).

Leave It to Mama

You get half a point if you have achieved "surrogate parental integration." You qualify if you are a red-hot liberal, passionately dedicated to racial justice and integration, worry a lot, read the *New Republic,* contribute to the NAACP—*but* live in a lily-white neighborhood in the suburbs. Meanwhile—and this is essential—your old mother, unburdened by any convictions whatsoever as to racial integration, bearing plenty of old-world prejudices and fears about non-Jews, possessing little education, not knowing the NAACP from the A&P, without benefit of the *New Republic* or clergy—SHE lives in the old "changed" neighborhood in Brooklyn, Cleveland, St. Paul, or Los Angeles with warm and human personal relations, happily complaining about her children to all her neighbors with no distinction as to race, color or creed. For this you get a half point (but you don't really deserve it). To get it up to three, move in with MOM.

The Party Line

Five points for having a live Negro at a party (although you lose half a point if he is light-skinned and a full point if he has a Jewish wife). You get a plus of one point if you have a different Negro at each succeeding party. Fair is fair. It is comon knowledge that a

Negro social worker in Great Neck (light-skinned, it is true, but better than white nonetheless) was totally used up within six months by Jewish party-givers on Long Island. It is rumored that at the end of the six hectic months, during which he gained fifteen pounds and became badly addicted to cheese blintzes, he joined the Black Nationalists (whom he despised) merely to find some peace.

In having a Negro at a party, you get a minus one for the gaucherie of involving him in any discussion of black power, unless of course he happens to be either anti-Negro or anti-white, which gives the party a special flagellant spice. In general, Negroes at parties should be involved in discussions about how the damn hippies litter their grass on the grass at the public park.

Integrate the Train

Six points for riding with a Negro on the commuter train. It is not required that you talk to him. That would be unnatural on a commuter train and would indicate that you are straining at racial liberalism, which, of course, is verboten. Be cool. Read your paper. Let him read his. Do your own thing. The important thing is to sit side by side and, together, glower at anybody who seeks to disrupt the ride with conversation. The commuter train, as every commuter knows, is no place for conversation and since you wouldn't talk to a white, don't talk to a Negro either. Just sitting there silently together is the most eloquent rebuff to the patterns of racial segregation in suburbia. Action speaks louder than words. Don't let some other liberal, seeking points, try to crowd in with you two on a three-seater. That's piracy and to be condemned. Let him find his own Negro. If your Negro finds it necessary at some point to move to another community, move with him. You will find that there are not enough Negroes living in suburbia to go around, and the federal government is not in a position to provide them as grants-in-aid.

Stay Loose

You get five points for maintaining good relations with Negro leaders in the community, six if you say "black" and not "Negro," seven if you can keep track of who the current black leader is without a scorecard (the latest angry black man to get in front of a television camera). Being a white liberal in race relations requires ever-increasing alertness and flexibility and a wet finger to the wind.

Stanley Nuchshlepper is a white liberal case in point. Warm-hearted, decent, sympathetic, a lover of all men, eager to please, Stanley was elected president of the local NAACP chapter. But two years later young black militants took over the group and denounced white leadership of civil rights groups as "bourgeois racists." Stanley promptly burned his president's scroll and issued a statement denouncing himself as a "honkey bourgeois racist" and pointing out that "black is beautiful." The year before that, Stanley had led an integrated group of pickets, fighting for integrated schools. They succeeded in getting the segregated Negro school closed down and put through a plan to bus the black kids into white schools. Stanley's picket sign then said: "DOWN WITH SEPARATE AND EQUAL." The following year, Stanley joined the new black nationalist leaders picketing to get rid of the bussing and to open up the black school as a bastion of black power: "UP WITH 'SEPARATE BUT EQUAL'; DOWN WITH RACIAL INTEGRATION." Stanley is now against civil rights and white liberals and he is for the black liberation struggle. He doesn't mind in the least that the black liberators make him picket by himself on the other side of the street from them. ["After all, I'm colorless."] To be a white militant, you must be with it, like Stanley, stay loose, keep the objective clearly out of mind, and be prepared to change flight in mid-somersault. If things don't get better, you may have to threaten to burn your own house down. After all, a pogrom is a pogrom.

Lend-Lease

You get six points if you are a Jewish housewife in the suburbs and you hire a domestic so she can take care of your house while you work as a volunteer at the day care center, taking care of her children.

Integrate Your Children

The real harvest of brownie points comes in living an unselfconsciously integrated life, enjoying racial and cultural diversity. The best evidence of such a relaxed liberalism is your own children. If, upon going off to college, your child shares a room with a Negro lad (if your child, that is, happens to be a boy; otherwise, fend for yourself) you earn three points. If he is free enough to take a Negro girl on a date, you get nine points. If he marries the girl, you, of course, hit the jackpot—and *plotz** on the spot!

* Faint dead away.

12. How to Raise Children, They Should Go to College

Getting Harold from the cradle to the college is the mission of Jewish parents and requires several intermediate steps. Here are some of them:

Surround the Child with Relatives

Because the Jewish birth rate in America is low, each new-born Jewish child has, statistically, only 1.7 siblings. This is not enough to work up intricate human relationships and even a decent sense of competitive rivalry. So we bring in the cousins, the aunts, the grandparents and the second echelon relatives whose names Harold will never remember, but whom he will be expected to kiss at weddings and Bar Mitzvahs. Mix all together and call it a mishpachah. Don't forget Aunt Essie, now approaching sixty, who must on no account be disabused of the notion that she was once Nikolai Lenin's paramour. Before he is one year old, Harold should be carried to the regular meeting of the Family Circle. This is important because, when he reaches maturity, he will go to the Circle meetings only by dint of the same mode of transportation.

Especially Grandparents

Grandparents are vital, particularly if they have an immigrant background. These old folks are the cement which holds the large families together; when the grandparents die, centrifugal forces go to work immediately to disintegrate the union which the oldsters compelled by the sheer force of character. It is the *bobbe* (grandmother) and the *zayde* (grandfather) who have lived in America for fifty years but still carry the flavor of Minsk and Jhitomir and Warsaw and Kiev in their very bones who, by their being, provide a living link to the centuries. They—and not the bland textbooks of the religious school—make history sing and cry and dance. Their memories of the *shtetl*, the intense Jewish ghettoes of Eastern Europe, trip a faint realization in the grandson that his own roots go deeper than Shaker Heights, deep into a sacred soil now covered by the volcanic ashes of a tortured history. In assessing the warm solidarity of the Jewish home in the knowledge that 85 per cent of American Jewry is native-born, one can only mourn the imminent passing of the zayde and the bobbe. If the new technology could somehow preserve them so that at least one would be available for every unborn Jewish child to come, the Jewish family would retain a salt and a zest which will be hard-pressed to survive the mod, youthful, fortyish, swinging, henna-haired American-born grandmother rushing from the mah-jongg board to the cha-cha lessons between trips to Aruba.

This is not to say that keeping the bobbe and zayde happy is not a challenging task. It is a Jewish game requiring exquisite patience. In the first place, they are not "happy"; they do not regard happiness as the goal of living. At best, they are "satisfied." But satisfaction requires a great deal from the children and the grandchildren, including: hourly telephone calls (So what's new, darling? . . . What should be new, I talked to you an hour ago); weekly visits; regular attendance at all Family Circles; unflagging interest in the colitis problems of Cousin Max who lives in South Africa and has not been in America for forty-five years; an understanding that if things are too good, that's bad; a willingness to break one's teeth in marshaling the small corps of Yiddish words still at one's command; spending an entire afternoon watching TV soap operas with the bobbe or an evening watching wrestling matches with zayde (the fact that he believes the matches are fixed in no way diminishes his ardor); breaking the Yom Kippur fast on the bobbe's chicken soup and challa (bread); and offering up the fidgeting grandchild for grandparental review BEFORE the first date, the Bar Mitzvah, the Confirmation, the solo at the dance recital and the bit part in the temple play. It is also necessary to check in with the bobbe before leaving on a weekend trip and at the precise moment of return. ("We're home, Mama. Now can we take off our skis?") To fail at any of these essentials is to leave the grandparents "disappointed" (an English word they pronounce as if it were Yiddish). To fail at all of them is to make them "very disappointed." What the children and grandchildren experience in THAT event one would not want to wish upon his worst enemies.

Bring Out His Talents

Any conceivable talent lying latent (or imagined) in Harold must be detected, irrigated and cultivated. This requires lessons in violin, ballet (what do you MEAN, it's not for boys?), piano, guitar, lapidary (Harold was first stoned at the age of ten), Hebrew, Spanish, tennis, painting and Byzantine architecture. A fierce and exhausting commitment to education and creativity is the hallmark of the Jewish home. The role of the parents is to: a) pay and b) shlepp (read car pool) the kids to their lessons. If the family is large enough, this may require both parents and two cars, operating in tandem and strictly by split-second timetable around the clock. Every hour on the hour the reluctant culture vulture must be shlepped to the waiting lesson. What all this does for the development of Harold's talent is well known (it makes him a cultured neurotic), but less well known is what it does for mom ("There are days when I wish we weren't Jewish").

Teach Him What it Means to be a Jew

There are several things that modern Jewish parents secretly resent about their own kids: 1) *they* didn't suffer through the Depression ("You eat every drop; you don't know what it is not to know where the next meal is coming from"); 2) *they* didn't live through the birth of the State of Israel and *they* act as if Israel is just another country in the Middle East ("Now we're going to see *Exodus* for the third time. This time, dammit, you'd better cry"); and 3) *they* didn't know Hitler. Indeed, they regard Hitler as a distant tyrant located somewhere in history between Haman and George C. Wallace. We can't really recreate these historical events for our kids (and we don't want to), but at least we can teach them what it means to be a Jew and what anti-Semitism is all about. (Unfortunately, for many Jewish parents the two are rigidly linked.)

How do we do it? It's not easy, particularly since practically none of our kids experience it for themselves. Fortunately, it is no longer a learn-it-yourself experience, as it was a generation ago.

We recently smuggled a tape recorder into the home of Mr. and Mrs. Govakind of Shaker Heights, Ohio, and recorded the following unedited conversation at the dinner table after a pleasant Sabbath dinner:

Father: "Children, I hope you realize how much we have to be thankful for—health, a good home, happiness . . ."

Mother: "And the fact that your grandparents are alive and well . . ."

Father: "Yes, you know, when I was your age things weren't so easy . . ."

Harold: "Oh, oh, here comes the Depression again."

Mother: "You stop that, Harold! Show a little respect for your father! He suffered plenty to be able to bring you up the way we do. Why, did you know . . . ?"

Father: "*I'm* talking, Alice. Did you kids know that when I was your age . . . ?"

Daughter: "You had to help support your entire family of eight. We know, Dad."

Father: "Shut up and listen! It's important for you to know what it means to be a Jew! When I was a little boy, growing up in Fargo, I used to get up at five every morning—FIVE O'CLOCK!—to deliver newspapers. And nobody had to lift me out of bed the way we do with certain children at eight o'clock! It was so cold my mother used to sit me on the hot radiator when I came home, and she would rub my feet and cry. Do you understand that?"

Harold: "Pop, don't forget the thirty-below-zero jazz. That's really cool. Get it?"

Father: "One morning as I put my papers in my sack, three young hoods surrounded me. 'Hey, are you Jewish?' they asked me. 'Yes, I am,' I said. Now, I want you kids to learn something from that. Never deny yourself. Stand up for yourselves as Jews. Be proud. Don't take any crap from anybody. . . ."

Mother: "Honey, your language!"

Father: "Sorry. Never take abuse from anyone. 'To thine own self be true, thou canst not then be false to any man.' That comes from Bialik, the great Jewish poet."

Daughter: "That's Shakespeare!"

Father: "Let it be Shakespeare. Where was I? Oh yes, in Fargo. I didn't chicken out, even though I was badly outnumbered."

Harold: "You stood there and fought like Judah Maccabee, right, Pop?"

Father: "Actually, I hit them with my paper sack and

ran like hell. But there's a lesson in all this. Which of you can tell me what it is?"

Harold: "Don't go anywhere without a paper sack."

Daughter: "Don't get up at five in the morning."

Be sure to teach him how to detect an anti-Semite at fifty paces ("I admire the way you Jews stick together. If only us white people could do that . . ."). And also how to put the anti-Semite down. He may never use this information and in the heat of a real incident, he will act from the viscera anyway, but it will make *you* feel better!

Give Him a Positive Jewish Education

This is more wholesome and crucial than the purely negative teachings about anti-Semitism. If a Jewish parent wills it, there is a way: bribery. If Harold will stay in religious school until the age of thirteen, give him a swinging Bar Mitzvah party and stop sequestering his *Playboy* (and also let him quit ballet). If he stays on until Confirmation (sixteen), give him access to the car by day. If he stays with post-Confirmation class, let him quit piano, buy drums, quarantine the Family Circle, drop his semi-annual visit to the barber, go to the Dodgers sports camp in the summer and save up for his own motorcycle. (Don't tell bobbe.)

But now the time has come to concentrate all your attention—and energies—on the paramount task of getting Harold into the right college. More than 85 per cent of Jewish youngsters get into and complete college, and Harold should not skew up the curve.

Getting Him Into College

The game of worrying about the child's college education begins at birth, becomes serious at kindergarten, the plot thickens with junior high school and becomes downright grim with high school. ("Now every grade counts toward college, turn off the TV.") Panic sets in during the junior year. ("For heaven's sake, you'll be in college in eighteen months and we don't even know where you'll go yet!") A few Jewish high-school seniors become so distracted by the mounting pre-college turmoil at home that they fail to win graduation from high school. These hapless youngsters are quietly bundled off in the dead of night, as if they were going to an abortionist, to visit relatives in St. Louis.

But, for the average Jewish youngster who makes it, what college to seek? There are many considerations. It should be away from home both because the youngster prefers it and, by this time, the parents need it. It should be an excellent school with a good academic reputation. It should be near enough for easy visits. It should be in or near a city with a substantial Jewish community, and there should be a fair proportion of Jews in the student body. The latter is, frankly, a quixotic hope that the youngster will meet and date other Jewish young people. What all this adds to is simple: IVY LEAGUE. Getting Harold into one of the Ivy League schools is not quite so easy.

The next step in the game is to drop in on the guidance counselor at high school. He has Harold's transcripts and he knows which colleges Harold is likely to make. Shake the counselor's hand vigorously, as if you are already grateful for his kind assistance. Offer him a cigar. Admire his office. Drop a name or two, but not too obviously. ("I would have called on you earlier in the week, but I was away at this Arden House Conference on 'Whither America.' Dr. Pusey of Harvard was there with me. Nice chap, Nathan.") Once you are into the meat of the conversation, make it very plain that you do not want any special privileges for Harold. You only want him in an Ivy League college, that's all.

After the counselor has made it clear that you will be wasting your time and money applying to Ivy League schools, go home and talk to your wife. Begin by tearing down the guidance counselor. ("Nice fellow, but if he's a guidance counselor, I'm Casey Stengel.") Your wife will respond by tearing you down. ("What did you say to him? I'll bet you opened up your big mouth and spoiled Harold's chances.") Your wife will then persuade you that you didn't ask the counselor the right questions. Over Harold's heated and embarrassed objections, you will arrange to see the counselor again. With your wife. This time no cigar, no Pusey, but he still says no Ivy League.

Now it is time to visit the possible colleges drawn from Harold's wishes, and the counselor's guidance. Finally, you and your wife help Harold to send out the three applications. (The high school sets a rigid limit of three, perhaps in recoil against the memory of the fellow who applied to 317 colleges and ended up at a Mexican barber's college in Montezuma.) The first letter, of course, goes to Harvard. Harold is so furious that, for two weeks, he refuses to mail the letter. ("They'll just laugh at us," he protests. To which his mother replies, "Let them laugh till they choke. At least I can tell my friends we're waiting to hear from Harvard.") The second is to Boston College. ("It's not Ivy League, but at least it's Boston.") The third is Galsworth, the safe school, a small college in South Carolina.

Now, during the sweat of the waiting period, it becomes imperative to build one's defenses. When your friends ask you about Harold's applications, you name all three. Galsworth? they ask, arching their eyebrows. "Oh yes," you say, "you never heard of that? That's odd. A fine small school, like Oberlin or Antioch. In a way, we hope he decides to go there. You know, a small student body, about a thousand, where he'll get individual attention. Not like one of those vast, cold Ivy League schools, all status and flimflam, where the kid is positively anonymous. No, this is a fine-type old Quaker school. Good liberal tradition, interracial and all that. I understand they have more PhDs per capita than any small Quaker school in South Carolina. Those fancy Eastern schools with those yippies and hippies are badly overrated, you know."

Harold, finally, is rejected by both Harvard and Boston and accepted at Galsworth. Harold heaves a deep sigh of relief (he had begun to fantasy that he would be accepted nowhere) and, sensing your disappointment, reminds you of what you had told your friends about Galsworth. "Shut up and open that college admission book. We're sending three new applications tonight." Six months and six applications later, Harold is admitted to a fine-type college near Worcester, Massachusetts. Harold is thrilled. You are not displeased either. "After all," you tell your friends, "a Jewish boy belongs in the Northeast. Worcester is not Boston, but Massachusetts is still Massachusetts. Go send a Jewish boy to South Carolina, they don't even have a Hillel Foundation, you have to have your head examined. What will he get down there? Right away he's dating Quaker girls, eating ham and going to school with Ku Kluxers. No, thank the Lord, we were lucky—we got our first choice."

Raising your child to be a nachas machine and a college graduate takes ingenuity. See how you're doing:

1. I give my child

a) all the rope he needs.
b) a guilt complex.
c) violin lessons.
d) a pain in the neck.

2. I give my child piano lessons

a) to keep up with the Cohens.
b) because my parents left us the piano.
c) once.
d) You would rather he ran around the streets?

3. My child does well in school

a) compared to whom?
b) out of fear for his life.
c) to please his bobbe.
d) but I wouldn't give him the satisfaction.

4. Discipline in our home is

    a) non-violent.
    b) ridiculous.
    c) absent.
    d) opposed to capital punishment.

5. I handle the television problem by

    a) rationing TV time.
    b) watching with them.
    c) blowing fuses.
    d) locking the set in the vault.

6. I give my youngster a good Jewish education

    a) no thanks to my husband.
    b) He shouldn't stand there with his mouth open when somebody asks him a question.
    c) He should marry Jewish.
    d) Tell me, what's so *good* about it?

7. Loving grandparents has meant to my child

    a) eight Chanukah presents every year.
    b) alliance against the common enemy (Sam and me).
    c) sweet spoilage.
    d) no candy. ("I *know* I'm

a Jewish grandmother but, let's face it, you're a fat slob.")

8. Surrounding my child with relatives

a) provides a psychological cushion.
b) Some cushion!
c) You mean couch, don't you?
d) Drives him right up the wall.

9. Growing up in a happy Jewish home, my child

a) made a nice recovery.
b) became a Jewish self-hater. ("I'm sorry I was born Jewish, but it won't happen again.")
c) was proud and ten feet high.
d) was not happy.
e) wanted to be a rabbi. ("What kind of a job is *that* for a Jewish girl?")

10. You can be sure my kid will never become

a) a cowboy.
b) a hunter.
c) a jockey.
d) a cantor-educator.
e) grateful.

11. If I had it to do it all over again, I would

a) not.

b) not drive away until I actually saw him go *inside* the temple.

c) also give him saxophone lessons.

d) practice birth control.

e) make sure that Sam hit him more. ("The kid didn't need it but it would have been better for Sam.")

You get 8½ points for every correct answer, of any. If you score 90 or over, your child has grown up fine despite your efforts. If you score 70 to 90, we urge you to have another child and start from scratch. You can't do worse. If you score less than 70, ask *your* parents to take the test.

13. How to Endure the College Years

We Jews don't like to take yes for an answer. One of our fiercest dreams in America has always been to give our children the best education possible. During the Depression, Jewish parents who might not have been sure where the next meal was coming from were certain of this: the children would go to college even if their legs were broken and the family had to subsist on borsht for seven lean years.

Well, today that dream is virtually fulfilled. Whereas some 27 per cent of college-age youngsters in America are in college, the figure for Jews is closer to 85 per cent —and it's rising. The quota against Jews was long ago swept away by the surging tide of Jewish applicants.

Has this made Jewish parents ecstatic? You don't know Jews. We are panicked. The only thing we like about it is that college is better than Vietnam—but, except for that saving grace, college is dreadful. Indeed, thoughtful students of Jewish life regard the campus as "a disaster area for Jewish values." The campus is full of goyim of the opposite sex, sex, pot, anarchists and revolutionaries, rebels and militants, hippies and yippies —practically all alienated from the traditional values of church, synagogue and home.

The key to understanding Jews is that we are like non-Jews, only more so, and are therefore disproportionately represented in every single one of the above (and practically everything else you can name). So Jewish parents now find themselves straining and stretching to get the kid into a good college so that they (the parents) can spend the next four (or more) years sweating, worrying, and demanding that B'nai B'rith's Hillel Foundation "save my boy" and fantasizing how he is losing his Jewish identity, head, virginity, moral fiber, innocence and draft deferment. As we will see in the following letters from Harold, they aren't so wrong . . .

October 1

Hi folks—

School is cool. I have two roommates. One is a guy from Winona, Minnesota, son of a Lutheran minister. Would you believe he never met a Jew before? The other is a crazy cat from Greenwich Village. He seems to be here to organize the campus against American imperialism. (He says Vietnam is old hat, he is avant-garde and is already planning against the Thailand war). When I told him I did not think Nixon should be impeached, he called me a fascist fink. Between Thorsten asking me whether Jews believe in immortality (Do they? Please ask the rabbi and write me special delivery), and Tony asking me to pitch in for 500 Viet Cong flags, I can't study too well. Two bennies keep me up till dawn. The food stinks. So do the girls so far. What happens if you make out checks when your bank funds are exhausted? Will call Wednesday at 2:00 A.M. hope you're up.

Hal

October 3

Hal Darling—

We are very disturbed by your letter. The college had no right putting you into a dorm with boys like that. Tell Thorsten to keep his religion to himself—hasn't he heard of separation of church and state? Tony worries me. He sounds to me like a commie agent. If he starts up again, please, please report it to the dean. He's not Jewish, is he? Tony is an Italian name, but you never can be sure. Please, darling, be careful. I hope you're eating at least three good meals. Don't skip breakfast.

Dad says he put more money in your bank, but you shouldn't make checks when your account is out. The bank doesn't like it. I'm sending a salami, cookies and a subscription to the *Jewish World*. What were the two bennies do-

ing in your room all night? How many roommates do you have anyway? You're not letting
your hair grow long again, are you?

All our love.

MOM

November 5

Dear folks—

Sorry, long time no write. Working hard.
Thorsten is very nice, don't worry, he's not trying to convert me or anything. His sister visited
last week and I took her out to dinner. She
had never met a Jew before either. I'm becoming a regular ambassador to the Gentiles. Big
pioneer. Thorsten asks if we Jews believe in
original sin. Do we? Ask the rabbi.

The Vietnam war is hotter here than in Vietnam. Tony (he's Italian, you're right) is making
stink bombs to throw when a guy from the State
Department speaks here next month. I can't work
up much steam about Vietnam. I'm still interested in civil rights. Most of the kids think
that's passe. Tony calls me a recidivist and says
I'm "wallowing in the sentimental swill of yes-
terday's battle."

My hair is long. I also have a beard. Please
send some white sox. Could you get me a copy
of MARIJUNA PAPERS? Salud.

Hal

November 6

Hal dear,

Why do you want MARIJUANA PAPERS? I am sending you Steinberg's BASIC JUDAISM, which you will find more valuable. It may help to answer that fellow's questions. Also please join the Hillel Foundation. It is not healthy to spend too much time with your own roommates. Mix more, meet different kinds of kids—Jewish ones.

You know we are very liberal. I am a life member of the NAACP. But you didn't go to college to save the world. There will be time after. Negroes have waited for deliverance a long time; they can wait till you finish college. I am appalled by the stink bombs and if you don't tell the dean, I will.

Write right away. We're worried.

DAD

November 24

Dear folks—

Ingrid visited us again. She has that typically Scandinavian attitude toward life—open, giving, honest. I really like her. I'm teaching her the hora, she's teaching me bundling. Don't worry, it's platonic.

Tony and I have worked out a compromise. We are combining civil rights and Vietnam. While Tony is throwing the stink bombs from the top of the administration building, I will lead a chorus of twenty blacks (we had to get seven from town, we only have thirteen on campus) singing: WE BLACK MEN WILL NO LONGER BOMB/OUR FELLOW COLORED RACES IN SOUTH VIETNAM! What a scene it will be! Some of the pro-Viet students are planning to surround the State Department guy and protect him. They want to stand up for the underdog. Those squares are real avant-derriere.

The salami came and went. I didn't want to smoke MARIJUANA PAPERS, just read it. Don't you trust me? The Steinberg book is very good, according to Thorsten, who is on Chapter 9. Hey, maybe we'll convert *him!*

Harold

Harold!

We are coming up this weekend, even if it is not Parents' Week. You are positively forbidden to participate in the stink-bombing. If you get caught, you will never be able to work for the government, or any industry connected with government, and it will not do Dad's business any good to see your face in the New York *Times*. (By the way, we got the picture. Your face looks thin. Please eat!)

Is bundling what we think it is? It is really too bad that we never had that talk we planned. Until Dad talks to you, stay away from that

Swedish girl. It is true they saved Jews during the war, but you are very young for Scandinavian customs. Do you still have that beard? The rabbi asked. We don't care. After all, you're a big boy. If you want to look like a donkey, that's your problem. You didn't mention your school work. See you Saturday.

All our love,
MOM

Dear folks—

I am in love with Ingrid. She is everything I ever dreamed of—and more. Don't think I'm betraying my faith. Her father has promised that, after he finishes the wedding ceremony, he will not interfere with my religious choice. We will let our children make up their own minds. No doubt you are shocked by all this, and I'm sorry. But this is a changing absurd world, and I dig it.

Don't bother to come up this weekend. By the time this letter comes, we will have occupied Earl Hall, converted Administration into a housing project, the stink bombs will have been fired and the Black Power chorus will have exploded all over campus. The joint will be crawling with FBI. Tony, Ingrid and the twenty blacks and I will leave the campus immediately after the demonstration and will hide away in a cave in the Berkshires. Don't try to find me.

Ingrid and I will be wed up there. Please don't hate me. I must live with my own conscience.

Harold

P.S. I must add this postscript before Dad has a heart attack and Mom cuts me off without a cent. There is no Ingrid, no Tony, no Thorsten and no twenty-Negro chorus. I made up the whole schmier to keep from telling you my grades. I'm flunking—French, chemistry and Revolution. But, as you now know, it could be worse. When you come up on Saturday, bring another salami and some more money.*

* With apologies to Jan Goodsell, syndicated columnist for Press Associates, whose column inspired this series of letters.

Epilogue: How You, Too, Can Be Jewish

If America is truly becoming Jewish, where does that leave the non-Jew? In *galut* (exile), perhaps? Must he mope around the periphery of things, his head hanging, wondering what "farblunjet" means? Is there no way for a non-Jew to get with it, to become part of the scene, to share in the action?

One way is to convert to Judaism. But it isn't easy. You see, Jews are used to being the *object* of conversions, not the *converters*. It's been three thousand years since Jews had a missionary program to the Gentiles, and that's a long time between acts. During those three thousand years it's been a one-way route: Christians have tried to save Jewish souls by such choice devices as persuasion, coercion, attrition and burning at the stake.

The net result: Gornisht helfen. Even when they were forcibly converted, Jews became Marranos (Christians on the outside, Jews on the inside) and surfaced again generations later when the pressure eased. So Jews have become allergic to missionaries and eager for a bombing pause.

Yet, while no Jewish Billy Graham will whip you into a frenzy of decision at Shea Stadium, and no little old Jewish lady will accost you in the park with a tract in her hot hand and a gleam in her eye, you can convert to Judaism if you wish to do it on your own steam. A growing, but still small, number of Christians have done it (usually because they are marrying Jewish spouses). But you'll find it an uphill fight to get in.

If a missionary is a fisher for souls, Jews are the peculiar fishermen who sit around in the boat, taking the sun, without rod, reel or bait. If a fish flops into the boat, they are surprised and more likely than not will throw it back. The way it works is that the would-be convert, having consulted the yellow pages, finally finds a rabbi (who doesn't make house calls). He calls on him at his study and tells him what he wants. Does the rabbi kiss him on both cheeks and circumcise him into the tribe on the spot? No. The rabbi cross-examines him. Tell me, why do you want to do this? Are you sure you understand your motives? Do you understand the consequences? Do you understand about anti-Semitism, how you will be perceived by your own relatives and Christian friends? Are you sure you are not trying to punish someone, maybe your parents? Have you ever been in a mental institution? In other words, man, are you out of your skull? Just as Groucho Marx wouldn't belong to any country club that would have him for a member, so Jews tend to suspect that anyone who wants to sign up voluntarily must be as schizy as a fruitcake.

If the cross-examination doesn't chase the seeker, then the rabbi assigns to him a truckload of books on Judaism (at least two of them authored by himself) and a regimen of study which would send any born Jew screaming into the night. Anybody who survives this academic obstacle course demonstrates that he has the minimum degree of masochism, loyalty and staying power required for membership in the Jewish people. He (or she) is then inducted in a moving conversion ceremony at the temple and, inevitably, becomes a more knowledgeable and active member than 96 per cent of the Jews who make it the easy way. And, of course, forty years hence the convert will still be identified by some Jews as that meshugener goy.

So maybe you would prefer to forego conversion and become a Marrano? This, too, can be arranged. One way is to marry a Jewish spouse (without conversion and, for the male, without adult circumcision). This permits you to splash around in the warm, ambiotic fluid of a Jewish mishpachah without portfolio.

But Jews are in short supply for this kind of massive program and, besides, the Jewish community would even rather have Christians try to *convert* them than *marry* them. I mean, we don't mind going to school with them, etc.

Another way is to borrow the Jewish life style. Having long since appropriated the Jew's religion, Christians are now busily absorbing the Jewish folk culture. You may have no option. Jewish humor and folkways are becoming as much a part of the air we breathe as, say, automobile fumes.

So, without becoming a card-carrying Jew, you can become—in the words of Pope John—a spiritual Semite, a fellow traveler, a pseudo-Marrano. You can have rapport, be plugged in to the right wavelength, develop internal radar and antenna, get smashed at Bar Mitzvahs and enjoy the vagaries and splendors of Jewish life as if you truly deserve it. The minimum requirements for such fellow-traveling are: 1) the right attitude; 2) some key words.

The right attitude should include the following:

Be Optimistic About the Future

Judaism is an optimistic faith and Jews have always had less to be optimistic about than anybody. The situation at any given moment can be summed up in two words: oy gvalt! Jews are optimistic because they figure, how can things get worse, and anything anybody does will be an improvement. Remember the difference between a pessimist and an optimist. An optimist is one who says this is the best of all possible worlds. A pessimist is one who fears that it is.

Never Despair of Improving the World

This is the quintessential Jewish task. Even in the darkest hours, Jews have believed it was their task to help make the world a better place for all men. Looking at the world today, it is obvious man could not make it much worse. It is like the sad occasion when a famous Yiddish actor died on the stage. A man in the balcony shouted down, "GIVE HIM AN ENEMA!" The manager said: "But he's dead. What good would that do?" Replied the man in the balcony: "It wouldn't HURT!" It wouldn't hurt to give the world an enema today. It is constipated with hatred, war and discord. Jews are, by some alchemy of history, the born doctors and analysts to the world—the enema of the people.

Maintain Your Zest for Life

Jews are crazy for life. When a Jew dies, Jews recite the Kaddish, a special prayer which doesn't mourn the dead. It sanctifies life and glorifies God. The essential Jewish toast for every happy occasion is *l'chayim*—to life! In a world obsessed with darkness and death, the Jewish reverence for life can be tonic. Jews don't dig the monastery-celibacy-retreat bit. (Hunting they can do without also.) They prefer to see life as a large, tangy lox-cream-cheese-onion-toasted-bagel sandwich, to be held in the hands, savored, tasted, enjoyed, licked and consumed. Recently, a dying young Jewish man left instructions for his mother to have his body packed in ice after death and stored away for possible restoration to life in a future medically advanced century. Possessing a Jewish spirit, he sensed that nothing in life is as absurd as death. Being a Jewish mother, she said who needs it, and proceeded to do what her boy told her to do. The boy's dream is no doubt meshuga. But, if he should pull it off, can't you just see him reincarnated in the twenty-fifth century, writing monographs on *A Living Judaism* or *Dying Can be Cool—God's Frozen People?* In the meantime, anyone for life on the rocks?

Cultivate a Special Relationship with Your God

Jews have a peculiar relationship with the Almighty. It is not, as some people think, that Jews are God's Chosen People. If we were chosen, what was the vote? No indeed. Most Jews believe their ancestors didn't volunteer for the Covenant at all but were drafted by God only after all other peoples hid behind the barn murmuring, "On us you shouldn't depend." Jews, therefore, don't see themselves as a superior or chosen people. But they do have an unusual relationship with Him. In the first place, they don't try to define Him. Secondly, they don't go around announcing His obituary—that's for Protestants. Thirdly, they think they have their place and He has His place, and they don't scapegoat God every time something goes haywire in the world. But, fourthly, and perhaps most important, they battle Him all the way. It's like a test of wills, a millennial lover's quarrel resounding down the centuries. You would think, one word from the Lord, and Jews would get cracking. But you don't know Jews. Abraham played one-upmanship with God in bargaining with Him as to how many just souls were enough to save Sodom and Gomorrah. Moses and God nudged each other half out of their minds. Jonah got wind of what God wanted him to do and he went whoosh into the foamy brine. God poured His plagues onto Job and Job only said, in effect, "Sock it to me, God—I wouldn't give you the satisfaction of yelling uncle." The relationship between God and the Jewish people is complex, swinging, ornery, reciprocal and infuriating. And it's not always the people's fault, either.

There but for the grace of God goes God and, let's face it, He is something of a Jewish mother Himself.

Always Answer a Question with a Question

Why? Why not?

Buy Copies of This Book . . .

and give them to all your friends and relatives. This will not do you a bit of good, but it will be very good for the author. And he's Jewish.

And, of Course, You Must Have at Least a Minimal Familiarity with Jewish Folkways

You should have picked them up in this book. If you are not already Jewish, check yourself in the following multiple-choice test to see if there is any hope for you:

1. Nachas machine

   a) A herring mayvin
   b) A snowmaker at the Concord
   c) A Jewish child
   d) A device to help you to think Yiddish and dress British

2. Hillel Foundation

   a) A girdle for fat Jewish girls
   b) An incomplete building, standing on one leg
   c) A program for Jewish college students

d) A religion dedicated to "To Whom It May Concern"

3. Yenta

a) An up-tight female yent
b) Hebrew for Arabs are lousy lovers
c) A cross between nudje and kochleffel
d) Harry Golden

4. Cultural Pluralism is

a) marriage between a Litvak and a Galitzianer.
b) seeing Fiddler twice.
c) each group doing its own thing.
d) an ecumenical *mikvah*.

5. Yeshiva

a) A rite of circumcision
b) A Hebrew word for group travel
c) A school
d) Look who is trying to become a nobody

6. Dropsie

a) The Jewish industrialist from Milwaukee after whom the Suez Canal was named
b) A possuk-hunter

c) A Jewish College
d) Falling off the Wailing Wall

7. Farblunjet

a) A Sisterhood collation
b) A Polish transvestite
c) Going to the wrong Bar Mitzvah
d) As Freud said about being born a Gentile, not one Jew in a thousand has such luck

8. Mishpachah

a) Aramaic for: Is it good for the Jews?
b) Three rabbis at the wedding—his, hers, and the caterer's
c) What Harvard gains when it admits a Jewish boy
d) The first Jewish weight-watcher

9. Chasidim

a) Israel's CIA
b) Thou shall not park in the rabbi's space
c) The original Jewish hippies
d) Abdullah's revenge

10. Podhoretz

    a) A kosher-style hotel in Atlantic City
    b) Gaelic Hatikvah
    c) Making it with *Commentary*
    d) Opening a can of worms at a luncheon meeting

11. Mazel Tov

    a) Hebrew for gesundheit
    b) What's Jewish about a sauna bath?
    c) Congratulations
    d) You call Brown a Jewish name?

12. Buber

    a) A Yiddish grandmother
    b) Booboo as pronounced in Brooklyn
    c) I-Thou
    d) A forty-one-year-old ex-shul president

13. Yom Kippur

    a) Close the window, can't you see it's raining?
    b) A Jewish fish
    c) A fast day
    d) A slow day

14. Simcha

    a) A Jewish car
    b) A Jewish poet

c) A happy event
d) An intravenous ordination

15. Chutzpa

a) Preaching a sermon without using the word "relevance" even once
b) Giving *Portnoy's Complaint* as a Bar Mitzvah gift
c) When a boy kills his parents and says you are obligated to give him alms because he is an orphan
d) Skinny-dipping in the Suez Canal

16. Nosh

a) A gay-gay discotheque in Tel Aviv
b) A cross (you should pardon the expression) between a fish and a knockwurst
c) Eat, eat
d) Yes, ladies, we do devein your shrimp

17. WEVD

a) A Jewish birth control pill

b) Hebrew for a pox on Philip Roth

c) A Jewish radio station in New York City where both English and Yiddish are spoken in Yiddish

d) Jewish underwear

18. Mazel

a) What is put on a Jewish dog

b) For 2¢ plain

c) Luck

d) A good shmoos

19. Kochleffel

a) Up the Establishment

b) We never had it so good and that is bad

c) A pot-stirrer

d) Shlemiel, go back to Chapter 5

20. Nu

a) So what's nu?

b) So what?

c) So?

d) Not a job for a Jewish boy

You get five points for each correct answer. The correct answer in every case is c. If you got over 90, you are Jewish, whether you know it or not—and you were asked not to take this test, why don't you listen? If you got 70 to 90, you are a nochshlepper (a follower-after) and, with diligence, you may still make it. If you got less than 60, contact a Jewish friend. If you have no Jewish friends, you are a loser and your future is bleak. After all, you can't even make it as an anti-Semite in America if some of your best friends are not Jewish. If you cannot locate a Jewish friend, please contact the author. We are hoping to set up an ever-normal granary for surplus Jewish friends to be supplied by those who have more Jewish friends than they can feed. In any case, get with it. The games Jews play are available to everybody regardless of race, color, creed, religion or previous condition of servitude. They may be exasperating but they are also exhilarating. Oy, are they exhilarating!